OTHER BOOKS BY DUBRAVKA UGRESIC

A

MUZZLE

FOR

WITCHES

Merima Omeragić in conversation with Dubravka Ugresic

Translated from the Croatian by Ellen Elias-Bursać

OPEN LETTER

LITERARY TRANSLATIONS FROM THE UNIVERSITY OF ROCHESTER

Originally published in Croatian as *Brnjica za vještice* by Multimedijalni institut

First edition, 2024

Catalog-in-Publication data: Available.
ISBN (pb): 978-1-960385-25-3 | ISBN (ebook): 978-1-960385-26-0

This project is supported in part by an award from the New York State Council on the Arts with the support of the governor of New York and the New York State Legislature

Cover design by Luke Bird

Open Letter is the University of Rochester's nonprofit, literary translation press:
Morey Hall 303, P.O. Box 270451, Rochester, New York 14627
www.openletterbooks.org

Printed on acid-free paper in the United States

CONTENTS

Witch, old witch, how do you fly?
On a broomstick going by.

Witch, old witch, what do you wear?
Black old clothes and uncombed hair.

Witch, old witch, what do you eat?
Little green bugs and pickled pigs feet.

Witch, old witch, what do you drink?
Apple cider vinegar and midnight ink.

Witch, old witch, do you live in a house?
I live in a haystack, with a little mouse.

A

MUZZLE

FOR

WITCHES

A deformed perspective

You speak of a deformed optics in a key essay of yours—"A Question of Perspective" (*Karaoke Culture*, 2011). How much has this skewed perspective shaped your work?

First I need to set the record straight. In November, 1992, an article was published by a preeminent Croatian bard who claimed that I was "infected by a strangely deformed optics," and suffered from a "regrettable loss of perspective." So these terms did not originate with me. This kind of collegial diagnosis of my views on nationalism and the Yugoslav wars was effectively a declaration of open season on me and all those they deemed witches, dissenters, enemies of the people. But as we have kicked off our conversation with the bard's ophthalmological diagnosis, I will go on to say that I acquired my particular perspective very early on, though I was blissfully unaware that the way I was seeing things was skewed. I hadn't yet started first grade. I remember feeling vulnerable and longing for friends. The little girls from my neighborhood excluded me from their games. Maybe they'd heard that my mother was *from another country*, a *foreigner*. Sometimes they teased me by chanting: Bulgaria girl, Bulgaria girl! though they had no idea what Bulgaria was, nor what "Bulgaria girl" might mean. True, I didn't know myself. When Roma girls showed up on our side street, the girls teased them the same way they teased me: Gypsy girl, Gypsy girl! The message from the mean girls, who never became my friends, was that I was not like them. I, too, was a Gypsy girl, and this pushed me to identify permanently with others, with Gypsies, Blacks, foreigners, Bulgarians . . . It became a permanent mental tattoo I have been carrying with me since my earliest years. The sound of the childhood ordeal the mean girls put me through still jangles in my ear like an alarm. It's not the substance that matters, it's the sound. The sound alerts me to the substance, while the substance stays more or less the same: *Bulgaria girl! Gypsy girl! Fatso! Ho! Scum! Butterball! Bitch! Buttface! Retard! Slob! Commie! Creep! Asshole! Slut! Moron! Dork! Loser!*

Society dumped many feelings of otherness and alienation upon you when you were a child. Did you become a cultural dissident to survive?

It's really difficult to say which came first, the chicken or the egg. I was an attentive, hard-working student in school, the ideal pupil for every teacher. But whenever the teacher assigned us a poem to learn by heart, I'd choose a different one to memorize. I'd apologize, of course, oops, sorry, I didn't know . . . The teacher couldn't flunk me because I'd recite my poem flawlessly. That was one of those rare moments when I was given an A for defiance! Many years later I was awarded the Resistance Movement prize (*Verzetsprijs*) for *Culture of Lies* (1995). I should add that, sadly, I was its last recipient. The Dutch prize was awarded from 1949 to 1997 in memory of a group of Dutch artists who were resistance fighters. Most of them were murdered or met their end in concentration camps. One of the major undertakings of the group was to set fire to the population census. By burning the census they hoped to save the lives of Dutch Jews.

In Croatia, censuses and rosters—the lists of who belongs to which blood type or ethnicity—have always been popular. Those who kept track were the church bureaucracy, municipalities, offices for ID documentation such as passports, and neighbors. Rosters of suspicious surnames could be found on commemorative lists at Jasenovac, the largest concentration camp for Jews, Serbs, Roma, Croatian communists, and anti-Fascists in Croatia during the Second World War. Secret lists of suspicious surnames made the rounds again in 1971 during the period dubbed the Croatian spring. Even my student ID, known as an index, became a source of suspicion. There used to be two categories listed in one's index: citizenship and ethnicity. I entered the same thing for both: Yugoslav. A fellow student remarked: "In Croatia it's only Serbs who register as Yugoslavs." I was stung by her attitude, but didn't understand her at the time. Registering as a Yugoslav wasn't supposed to be a mark against you. I'm not certain of the precise number, but more than a million people in Yugoslavia registered as Yugoslavs in those days. True, out of Yugoslavia's population of twenty-four million this was not a large number, but it was large enough to show that there did exist the option of registering that way. Twenty years later, in 1991, her attitude surfaced yet again—because of Serbian nationalism and the collapse of Yugoslavia. I was, therefore, seen as a traitor long before the media and my colleagues at the School of Humanities and Social Science saw me that way. The lists of people declared traitors and enemies of the people were no longer secret in the 1990s. One's first and last name and telephone number were public—everything others needed for communication. This was how the ordinary citizens of Croatia could lend a hand by pestering traitors. After receiving harassing phone calls, I went to the post office several times to request that my phone number be switched from listed to unlisted. The company did not lift a finger to help. Croatian citizens became experts at exposing who was who. I remember when my mother's closest neighbor—with whom she drank coffee daily—once said: "My dear, those Bulgarians, aren't they really Serbs?"

If there hadn't been local experts on hand, eager to collaborate, Aleksandra Zec, a twelve-year-old girl from a Serbian family living in Zagreb—murdered in the first months of the war—might still be alive today.

In terms of literature, how and when did your dissident impulse arise?

My dissident impulse has always been there. The only problem is in the reading. To know what a dissident impulse is you need to be familiar with, have an ear for, the constellation, the cultural moment in terms of the local, regional, national, and global, and not only as all these pertain to literature, but also to politics and cultural policy. There were many things I was oblivious to back then and still am now. Hence why the word "impulse"—at least in terms of my first steps—feels so apt. The constellation was formed by the canonic authorities, the generational, collective, and cult authorities. Furthermore, Yugoslavia, as a country outside the Communist bloc, was open to the circulation of cultural information, to translations. There was a period when the country had a thriving publishing industry. When young, my literary generation, dubbed the Croatian Borgesites, was crazy about Borges and other literary icons of the day. That generation ended up embracing the profitable model of genre literature, mostly detective stories. I diverged from the generational path and, as a first-year student of comparative literature, quite unexpectedly, and, fortunately only briefly, strayed into children's literature. In my early years as a student, we admired Duško Radović, a Belgrade writer. Radović was a children's poet who raised the bar high with his marvelous verses. He inspired brilliant illustrators, the producers of children's television shows (*Na slovo, na slovo*— Onward to Letters!), children's gazettes, and stunning picture books. Radović was a sort of Yugoslav Dr. Seuss.

The high standards he set for children's literature later evaporated and the cultural climate of the 1980s in Serbia devolved to the bright and breezy style of popular writer Momo Kapor, known for his jaunty, vulgar quips. A writing style referred to as "jeans prose" took hold in Croatia, with novels inspired by *Catcher in the Rye* by J. D. Salinger, a model followed by writers of the generation slightly older than mine, whom we referred to as the "boys." Momo Kapor's brash misogynism caught hold. His vulgar humor was an only slightly more urban version of boorish Herzegovinian village chants, such as: "Hey, honey, pull down your pants, I'm on the train from Munich with it hot in my hand." This, then, served as the framework for Franjo Tuđman, Croatia's president, when announced to the general Croatian public how glad he was that "his wife was not a Serb or a Jew." Furthermore, his words set the stage for quips by Croatian intellectual Vlado Gotovac. When asked by a television reporter what sort of women he preferred, Gotovac replied, "Clean!" presumably with hygiene in mind. Bidding farewell to Croatian soldiers who were on their way to the front, Gotovac famously told them that their death *must be clean*, presumably with their moral purity in mind rather than their hygiene. Nobody commented on these statements as bizarre, or managed to recognize infamous Fascist vocabulary lurking in what was said. Indeed, many Yugoslavs were amused, and still are, by the popular question and answer: "Have you read Ivo Andrić's *Woman from Sarajevo*?" "Read her? No! I f---ed her!"

So, while we are on the subject of my clueless early days and dissident impulses, the crucial role in forming and articulating the position of the literary dissident, like always, is something that evolves within the general cultural climate of the place, the period, political praxis, trends, current thinking about culture and cultural praxis, the media, market politics, taste in art, the literary canon, the national and the transnational, and many other factors. I enrolled in comparative literature because I had already read widely in the Yugoslav literatures while I was still in secondary school and realized I had found a lot of it boring. Aside from Miroslav Krleža, Ivo Andrić, and Miloš Crnjanski, I hadn't come across much of anything that held my interest. I admit that my indifference was informed by youthful arrogance. I discovered literary theory and the culture of the Russian avant-garde and

European modernism as a comparative literature student and this quickly whetted my appetite for dissident impulses. I also read major contemporary writers of the older Yugoslav generation such as Danilo Kiš, Borislav Pekić, Bora Ćosić, and others, who, after Yugoslavia fell to pieces, abandoned their role within the Yugoslav literatures and were embraced by the canon of Serbian literature, either through their own efforts or the efforts of the ethno-nationalist critics.

There is an exceptionally interesting, exotic, and fleeting phenomenon that surfaced in Serbian literature and film. That it was fleeting, I should add, is to be expected, because every exotic literary departure or non-conformist gesture is quickly spent. Literature invariably reverts to the mainstream, or, better said, it seldom abandons the mainstream. For instance the only thing to have survived from the phenomenon of camp is the definition of camp that Susan Sontag so deftly articulated. Let us return to the local literary quirks, the sabotaging of values that provided the underpinnings for serious (Kiš) and mainstream literature. These quirks are part of what has been termed wild literature—mainly based on paraliterature. (Ivan Čolović, *Divlja književnost: etnolingvističko proučavanje paraliterature* [Wild Literature: An Ethnolinguistic Study of Paraliterature, 1985]).

I remember Miloš Jovićević, author of a slender volume with the title *Nevini muškarac* [An Innocent Man]. The media—with their appetite for oddball characters to share with the masses—stirred up a veritable firestorm over his novel that could be seen, perhaps, as a forerunner to autofiction, which is, simply put, the media term (though not a literary theory term) for autobiography. The author, Jovićević, was only semi-literate, a male virgin, obsessively in love with the star of a woman's basketball team who was twice his height. Had the way not been paved by *Kako je Dobrislav protrčao kroz Jugoslaviju* [How Dobrislav Ran Across Yugoslavia, 1977], a remarkable novel by professional writer Milovan Danojlić, perhaps readers wouldn't have had so much patience with Jovićević's semi-literate, bizarre story. In his novel, Danojlić expresses empathy for writers. They are all Dobrislavs, burning with the same creative fervor. The prospect of glory and success is merely a question of luck. But no matter what he does, success eludes tragicomic Dobrislav. A few years earlier, Ivo Brešan wrote the play *Predstava Hamleta u selu Mrduša Donja*, [The Performance of Hamlet in the Village of Lower Jerkwater] and Krsto Papić made the play into a movie in 1974. Moma Dimić penned the novel *Šumski građanin* [Forest Citizen]. Dimić's protagonist was a real person, a man named Radoš Terzić, a forerunner of today's reality TV, a total outsider who ultimately took Dimić to court because the author used him twice, for both the novel and for *Kako sam sistematski uništen od idiota* [How I was Systematically Destroyed by Idiots, 1983], a movie directed by Slobodan Šijan. Stanoje Ćebić's novel *Zašto sam postao vo* [How I Became an Ox] came out in 1982, a totally offbeat work by a true outsider. This constellation is worth remembering: first Yugoslav film noir, then the genius of Dušan Makavejev, and then Želimir Žilnik's virtuoso docu-drama. These were times of powerful social and political sensibilities. I found this sort of socialist camp unusually exciting, because it was, among other things, so unexpected.

While we're on the subject, where do you see the didactic potential for a resurgence of children's literature? Is subversion possible through children's literature? What stands in its way?

In terms of the adult canon, children's literature is already in and of itself an instance of literary subversion. Everything that makes a canon a canon—pomposity, the imprimatur of grand, universal themes—finds its parallel in children's literature, but the themes and literary strategies in children's literature may take on an ironic, parodic, subversive, and, therefore, more literary character. Children's literature employs far richer and more elaborate linguistic devices, from deliberate distortions of language through the use of folklore forms (such as nursery rhymes) to inventing new language (Khlebnikov's *zaum*) and introducing fantastical, absurd, and parallel worlds. In other words, children's literature primarily means freedom. The finest works of children's literature are masterpieces (from the fairy tales of folklore to *Alice in Wonderland, The Wizard of Oz*, and *Winnie-the-Pooh*), works every bit as important and valuable as Cervantes, Shakespeare, Dante. The best of children's literature is also a total subversion of the literary values of literature for adults. The Russian absurdists—the last Russian avant-garde group (Daniil Kharms, V. Vvedensky, Nikolay Oleynikov, and many others)—eked out a living as writers for children. Only later was it discovered that Kharms was as great in his absurdist texts as he had been in his poetry for children. What makes great children's literature so exceptionally appealing is its semantic elasticity.

And as far as didactic potentials are concerned, they surfaced with nationalism and the butchering of the Yugoslav cultural scene into tribal communities—Slovenian, Croatian, Bosnian, Serbian, Macedonian, Montenegrin, and Albanian. Nationalism is intellectual suicide. Every nationalism tsunami brings about an appalling provincialization of culture and everyday cultural praxis. In the post-Yugoslav context, one of the stories that confirms the didactic potentials of a resurgence of children's literature pertains to Branko Ćopić, a beloved Yugoslav writer who was adored by Yugoslav readers, who were eager for cheer and optimism in the years after the Second World War. And then the writer faded from view (Ćopić committed suicide). Ćopić's classic story for children, *Ježeva kućica* (*Hedgehog's Home*), a fable in verse, a fairy tale, a poem, became one of the classics of the Yugoslav literatures. It was published in countless editions and was included in the elementary school curriculum. With the collapse of Yugoslavia and the violent carving up of shared cultural property, however, *Hedgehog's Home* vanished from view. As Ćopić was a Serb, his *Hedgehog's Home* was thrown out of all the other ex-Yugoslav literatures and relegated exclusively to the Serbs. And then (some thirty years had to pass!) this totally innocent, traditional, didactic children's poem was brought back to the shared linguistic realm as a form of gentle protest against the brutal carving up of cultural property. Children's literature is often ideologically manipulative, because nobody questions its innocence. And furthermore many writers for children (and other writers, of course) from the periods I'm talking about, slid readily into nationalism at the moment when the summons was heard for national homogenization.

Women and the male perspective

You offered a critique of sexist culture in your short novel, *Štefica Cvek u raljama života* (*Steffie Cvek in the Jaws of Life*). Then the popularity of the movie, *In the Jaws of Life*, turned what had been your critique into a farce. Where were you and Steffie then?

I remember when the head of the Russian Literature Department at the School of Humanities and Social Sciences in Zagreb, a professor with whom I'd been working on the *Pojmovnik ruske avangarde* [The Glossary of the Russian Avant-Garde] project for many years, once said to me: "When will you start doing something worthwhile?" I asked him what that ought to be. "Why, literature!" he said. I answered that I was writing literature. The professor interrupted me: "I meant literary scholarship." How did it suddenly happen that *Steffie Cvek in the Jaws of Life*, a short novel that was, among other things, my exploration of the fundamental tenets of the Russian avant-garde, became, from the professor's academic perspective, an unworthy literary venture?

All in all, I learned my lesson that there is no doctoral degree or promising literary reputation that can shield women from men's fear and contempt, which is camouflaged in the more civilized settings, while it manifests itself as open misogyny in the less civilized ones. Yet most women seem to be incapable of recognizing misogyny. And if they do recognize it, then they prefer to opt for the traditional order of things for the sake of "peace at home." This mental oversight is both their good fortune and, at the same time, it prolongs their misfortune. For if women were to see misogyny for what it truly is, at a personal and global level, they'd sink into the earth from shame. It took me a long time to detect the syndrome of misogynistic behavior. Even men are not capable of detecting their own misogyny. Croatian poet Antun Šoljan wrote in 1991 that I'd be better off dabbling in literary knitting and crocheting (this being his reference to *Steffie Cvek in the Jaws of Life*) than politics. In other words, he contested my right to political thinking and public speech, meanwhile discrediting me as a writer. A young writer at the time, who has since matured into a significant literary arbiter, asserted that, sure, my essays were literate, but I should stick with *Steffie*. These and many other "intellectuals," in what is now "democratic" Croatia, fought for the freedom of speech. Whose?

The story that made the rounds that a group of travelers on a bus in Serbia worked themselves into a frenzy, chanting "I'll bang you, I'll bang you until your Aunt comes home from Bosanska Krupa"—a line from the movie *In the Jaws of Life* based on my novel—was supposed to be my greatest literary achievement. Yet ungrateful wretch that I am (!), I experienced these moments of local literary glory as a slap in the face, a confrontation with my own failure, with the impossibility of communication. I had troubles dealing with my feeling of internal defeat. In a word, I was young.

The widespread discreditation of women in the public realm of the academy and the art world is appalling. Mira Furlan declared at some point that *our film directors don't know what to do with actresses except undress them* . . .

In the autumn of 1991 in New York, I watched a video with my friend, Mira Furlan, a Croatian actress of film and theater, that was put together to present an overview of her filmography. The video was a collection of clips from the movies that had made her a Yugoslav movie star. The clips were agonizing to watch. Scene after scene of a meaty man's fist kneading a woman's bare breast, of lovemaking often ending in rape, a scene in which the actress tries to hang herself from a toilet chain and fails (ah, such a klutz!), scenes in which men showed no restraint when slapping her across the face. The video included a famous clip, remembered by many Yugoslav moviegoers, each for his or her own reasons, in which the husband bashes in the head of his wife, the actress, with a big rock, thereby illustrating the venerable folk custom of wife-bashing, the murder of an unfaithful woman (or someone elderly) by smashing them with a heavy rock, usually wrapped in felt. "Do not show this demo video of yours to anyone," I said. "Why?" she asked. "Imagine for a moment that you're someone here in the United States, watching these scenes . . ." I don't remember if we both burst into tears. I do know we grasped the true meaning of the phrase "deformed perspective."

Have you meanwhile changed your perspective?

I have retained my deformed perspective to this day. With satisfaction I have noticed that several young women share it, such as Lana Bastašić. In her story "Šuma" [Forest], published in the collection *Mliječni zubi* [Baby Teeth], she slays the traditional literary figure, the patriarch, the father figure, the omnipresent male authority, with a swift, well-aimed bullet. And while Camus's *The Stranger* begins with the famous sentence *Maman died today*, Bastašić begins her story with the sentence *Strangling Dad was going to take time.* The father in her story goes off every day to the forest to *clear his head.* The daughter discovers the real reason. He is sneaking away to masturbate.

And now to shift this perspective to the small realm of literature (and to ignore all others, especially politics) and examine the male literary canon. We can recall the ever-present male figures—the writers, literary historians, critics, editors, literature professors, prize jurors, literary cliques, representatives of the national literatures who even rose to become president of the republic or to serve in the diplomatic corps (there are too many examples throughout what used to be Yugoslavia to list them all)—the literary bureaucrats who decide who will and who will not enter the national canon; the ones whom they have dubbed the moral literary verticals and the ones who are not moral verticals; those who are our Homers and those who are not; the literary male exemplars who carry on dialogues and polemics with their *esteemed* literary *buddies*; who cultivate their literary sons while ignoring their daughters, especially a daughter who might one day venture into the forest and raise questions about the father's dignity and authority. Yet nonetheless most women in culture continue to respect, protect, and serve these fathers of theirs, exactly as if they are waitresses, instead of women using their brains.

True, men often coerce us into behaving like waitresses without giving this a second thought. Doing so is more often than not a reflexive gesture. Ours and theirs. Some twenty years ago I was on a panel with one of the classic figures from these literatures. As there was no translator available, they asked me to translate into English. He treated me exactly that way, as if I were his translator instead of his equal. I remember he was even a little irritated because, in his opinion, I wasn't keeping up with him. Or a fresher example, from a recent panel in New York where aside from me and another female colleague who is a professor at one of the universities in New York City, the other panelists were men, compatriots, "intellectuals." When the panel ended, one of them asked me to take a picture of *them*, the *panelists*. The boys lined up and flung their arms around each other and I snapped the photograph for history, which did not, of course, include my female colleague or myself. None of our colleagues thought to ask us to join them. I only caught on later, and thinking about this dredged up my memory of the boys in the snapshot, Croatian writers of the male sex. On the photograph they have their arms around each other and are wearing T-shirts with the commercial slogan "Read Croatia!"—a paraphrase of "Buy Croatia!" Hence, "Croatia" is imaginable and desirable but only as a category of gender. Male.

Society forms the prototype of the desirable woman. What sorts of societies are these, and what is our desirable woman like?

About ten days ago all the Croatian newspapers—from *Jutarnji list* to the local papers funded by the Ministry of Culture, tourist offices, and EU commissions—published an obituary for a *legendary* woman. The headline caught my attention, especially because I didn't recognize the name. It turns out that the woman had worked as an air traffic controller at the Zagreb airport. She had become a legend because she was the one who uttered words of welcome to two generals when they returned home from The Hague (from the International Criminal Tribunal for the former Yugoslavia) where they had been on trial for war crimes. All of this had nothing to do with the poor woman, but with the media who swiftly instrumentalized her death so they could yet again prod the public to remember these "heroes" of the Homeland War. The Croatian media has been entertaining its readers for the last thirty years with its top list of desirable and undesirable Croatian women. The result is that the only good Croatian woman is a dead Croatian woman, or one who is modest, submissive, quiet, and anonymous, hence, the proverbial waitress. And a waitress, if she does open her mouth, does so only to serve her male customers.

So why would men relinquish the privileges they have acquired and use?

Indeed, why would they? Did anyone remark on the story about the unfortunate air traffic controller? No, because there are too many similar stories, and it's impossible to process them all. This is why it's difficult to see the forest for the trees. This is why it is a challenge—behind the story about the air traffic controller—to perceive the policy of the systematic instrumentalization of Croatian women by Croatian men. I recall that thirty years ago young men in a small town stopped a young Roma woman, set fire to her skirt, and fled. The woman went up in flames, but passersby did manage to save her life. When journalists asked the Roma woman whether she would demand charges be raised against the young men, she said: "Goodness, why would I? They were just having a little fun!" Wise woman. She knew that even the finest attorneys wouldn't be able to defend her. All of our communities—whether Croatian, Serbian, Bosnian, or others—always step up to defend their local thugs.

No one thought to recall that a few hours after the innocent air traffic controller welcomed the generals, a group of students in Podstrana near Split celebrated the generals' return. On that occasion one of the young women from the group ended up in the hospital with gruesome injuries to her abdomen, intestines, uterus, vagina. The doctors at the hospital in Split said they had never seen anything like it. The young woman, the victim, couldn't remember a thing. Nor could the young man who'd raped her because he was drunk. The young man, "our boy Roško," was sentenced to four years in prison for inflicting grave bodily injury and eight months for sexual intercourse without consent. Roško then fled. When he was apprehended, his sentence was lengthened to six years. Long ago, rapists used to cut women's tongues off so they couldn't tell anyone what had happened. There was no need to cut the tongue off of the poor woman from Podstrana. The rapist, "our boy Roško" guaranteed her a peaceful life: amnesia and permanent disability.

Hasn't the vast number of well-educated women brought about a meaningful change in the way women and their role in society are perceived?

One's occupation, one's profession are secondary to physical appearance, though this applies only to women. The media set the bar and men and women continue to respect these male standards. Prominent attorneys, doctors, the wives of famous soccer players, female judges, and scientists are praised for the brand of purse they carry, for their clothing, their shoes, and especially for their good looks despite their advancing age, or their amazing recovery after giving birth, and, of course, for their husbands. Our newspapers report on this almost daily, and even the women who have broken through into the elite do not protest. Famous women in sports aren't valued for their athletic accomplishments until the moment when they make it known that they have had a cosmetic makeover. A woman on the hammer throw team must become "our prettiest hammer thrower" before a word about her competitive results is heard. Women doctors in Croatia first describe themselves in their professional profiles as wives, a mother of three sons, and only then state their specialization. Croatian women who play a prominent role in the media thereby demonstrate to the media-anonymous Croatian women what they need for success in life. Good looks and a successful husband. The one doesn't go without the other. All else matters far less. To be the wife of a successful man is already in and of itself—a profession.

The greatest moral nadir in academic standards wasn't reached when a professor's recent sexual harassment of a female student at Zagreb's School of Humanities and Social Sciences was made public. It happened when a female professor at the Zagreb University Law School invited legendary Yugoslav fashionista Žuži Jelinek to give a talk for the Law School's female students about how to catch a husband. Literally, *catch*. Because the fashionista, judging by her CV (public appearances, columns, and biography), was a major expert.

Women are a subordinated category: in the classroom—women writers *linger* as a token minority in syllabi/curricula—in student quotas (paradoxically higher), in jobs at the lower levels of elementary and secondary school teaching, moderators and promoters, but seldom do they work as more serious academic professors and scholars whose opinion is autonomous, relevant, and transformative. The struggle for survival within the stated boundaries implies a relationship that is dependent on the literary academic *pater familiases* and acceptance of compromise and a bought silence.

I remember the primers, anthologies, and histories of Croatian national literature. One of the most well-known authorities at the time was a professor who lectured on the history of Croatian literature at the School of Humanities and Social Sciences. In his historical surveys, Croatian literature was organized by epochs, and every epoch had its own literary exponents. These representatives were *exclusively* men. The surveys were illustrated by portraits of famous Croatian writers. At the end of each literary period one found a brief addendum (I'm quoting here from memory): *It should be noted that a few women writers were also active in this period, writing mainly for children.*

No one has ever—at least emotionally, if not intellectually—examined this data and data like it, just as nobody has taken on the job of trying to change this discriminatory cultural praxis. Perhaps because it is difficult admitting how discriminatory it has been. Female authors were simply not there, or barely there. And not a single professor has said that the big Croatian literary names were largely aping European literary models, which is fine, except that they did so with a lag of fifty to a hundred years. Do you find yourself wondering how writers were writing in Croatia (Serbia, Bosnia, etc.) when *Madame Bovary* appeared in France? Who were the big Croatian literary names at the time of European Modernism? Even these pitiful apers of literature, however, would not have existed had there been no women readers.

How to write and create as a woman if we have identified ourselves as culture's stepchildren?

It is entirely possible that gender-unaware women in post-Yugoslav zones are amenable to satisfying the fantasies men have about them. I hope there are women researchers who will prove otherwise. The same applies to the literary field. Have women literary critics with a feminist bent, female scholars, professors, publishers made an effort to initiate a praxis of reading male canonical texts through female eyes? *Male Croatian literature* continues to occupy its pedestal, though it isn't described as male, but simply as literature. The literature written by women is something separate, specific, about those women's things. This is why it is called *wo*men's literature. The term *women's* literature is discriminatory, just as the term *men's literature* would be, if anyone dared use it. And besides, though the theme of the so-called universalism of men's literature has long since been a subject in literary theory, it has not been the subject of literary praxis. So I am not sure whether there is any point in "re-warming" this aspect.

The same names have been circulating within Croatian culture for the last thirty years, as long as the nationalist mainstream has been on the rise. True, modern theories are being embraced, intellectual groups and "communities" are rising. Time and effort are needed if the system of patriarchal values is to be extirpated, as it has flourished over the last thirty years, while rooting itself ever deeper, in the fertile manure of nationalism. The environment in which they have developed has shaped men just as it has shaped women, and most men do not seem capable of grasping the idea of the equality of men and women. And it is also worth asking: how capable of this are most women?

The implanting of cultural memes

The post-Yugoslav countries are experiencing a precarious moment, a moment of populism, or, if I may, of neo-fascism, where *the intelligentsia is choosing whether to adapt, collaborate, or resist the overt, covert, and all other forms of terror.*

Populism, as the dominant political constellation—particularly in the countries spawned by ex-Yugoslavia and in the formerly Communist countries such as Poland or Hungary—has shown us all its pitfalls and threats. The same thing has happened with the recent US political constellation, known as Trumpism. Even people who are politically illiterate are well aware that with a populist government there will be less funding for culture, education, and health care, yet still they vote for populists without realizing that the consequence will be that their own children will be less literate than they are. And the more illiterate and powerless voters are, the better for the ruling class. The laws of the marketplace contribute their part to this. The market is dependent on the powerful media. Digital media, of course. Society changes, people change. Most people believe in global progress, few believe in the possibility of social barbarization, i.e., the return of the barbarians.

As far as culture is concerned, distinctions should be drawn at this point among terms. There is popular culture—the culture of mass media with its attention to market profitability—and populist culture that follows and supports populist policy. Terms such as elite culture need to be redefined, because the boundaries between culture and subculture, high and low, elite and commercial, authentic and imitational have blurred. The notion of canon should be redefined, to see how much relevance that term still holds. It would seem that the traditional role for the arbitrator of good taste has been abandoned, and now anyone can step into this role. There is no longer any critical writing designed to teach us how to read a literary text, perhaps because few know how to explain what a literary text is any more, or perhaps because critical thinking no longer matters. All in all, traditional arbitration has disappeared and has been replaced by the far mightier arbitration of the *market*, behind which is masses of readers. Today's literary authorities are growing out of a robust collaboration between the media and publishing, from social media (Facebook, Twitter, and so forth) and the astral positioning of people in culture, who used to be deemed the intellectual elite in times gone by. Writers, too, position themselves as the authorities, arbitrators, those who are in the know.

Can post-communist cultures be said to have been compromised?

As far as the cultures of the post-Yugoslav countries are concerned, yes, they are seriously compromised. Because how can a culture founded on the principle of ethnic exclusivity call itself a culture? How is the Croatian cultural herd marked? By culture or by blood type? Or are those two actually one and the same thing? Culture implies inclusivity. The ethnic exclusivity upon which Croatian culture has been proudly built for the last thirty years implies the destruction of everything that is not true to blood type, hence ideologically "ours." How could anyone morally survive the burning of books and systematic cleansing of Croatian libraries of non-Croatian books without dying of shame or at least speaking out in protest? Few people in the Croatian community have breathed a word about this. If writers were so scared (Who has scared them so badly? Their newly won democracy?) why haven't teachers, university professors, journalists protested? What about the librarians who took part in destroying books? This case would have been completely forgotten if not for a handful of journalists who did write about it (while writing for *Feral Tribune,* the opposition journal). There were two or three writers, and then there was Ante Lešaje, a retired professor of economics who dedicated his retirement to writing a magnificently relevant book, *Knjigocid: uništavanje knjiga u Hrvatskoj 1990* [Librocide: The Destruction of Books in 1990s Croatia].

Young readers don't get this. They think it has nothing to do with them—all of it happened before they were born.

When I was young, I too felt that local stories calling for redress were boring. Still, for those who might be interested, here is a brief recap. In 1992, the Ministry of Education, Culture, Sport, and Science formed a working group that laid out guidelines for librarians, under the heading *Fundamental Principles for Revising School Libraries.* The guidelines instructed librarians on how to put the fundamental principles into effect. In brief, they explain that libraries may be used for books whose authors and translators are Croats. All the books must be printed in the Croatian language and only in the Roman alphabet. School libraries must not keep books which are ideologically tinged. School libraries must not keep books by writers who are of non-Croatian ethnicity. Thanks to journalists from *Feral Tribune*, the secret document was made public. The Ministry, with the Minister at the time at its head, distanced themselves from the *Fundamental Principles*, although the Minister did come out and say publicly that Croatian literature could only be taught in schools by Croats. The librarian at the Nikola Hribar school in Zagreb's suburbs had meanwhile destroyed 400 books. The Culture Center in Slatina burned 2,000 books. The director claimed he was acting on the Ministry's instructions. Soon a conciliatory gesture appeared in the form of stickers with a Croatian interlace design that would serve to distinguish the Croatian books from the non-Croatian books. The director of the Miroslav Krleža Lexicographical Institute publicly boasted that 40,000 sets of the Yugoslav Encyclopedia had been pulped. One of the Zagreb librarians appeared on television in 1994, saying that he himself had seen to it that unsuitable books were cleared off the shelves of his library. A librarian from Korčula destroyed 500 books. The former Finance Minister announced in 1998 that a higher sales tax for books should be introduced, so that the funds raised by the tax could be used to finance the clearing out of Croatian libraries of books printed "in Serbian and similar languages."

I only started following the situation with books and libraries in 2000. By that time apparently almost three million books had been destroyed. The Nikola Hribar librarian still had his job at the same school. The Korčula librarian had been promoted, after she destroyed books, to be director of the Korčula library. The author of the *Fundamental Principles* was issued a pro forma suspension in 1992, but continued receiving her salary until she was named director of all Zagreb libraries. All this happened a long time ago. The only thing I remember is that the best-sellers at the time were books by Paulo Coelho and Hitler's *Mein Kampf.*

Why dredge up with such vehemence this inconsequential story of contemporary Croatian history? Precisely because of the fundamental principles for revision. New Croatian culture (which at first proudly sported the propaganda badge of their "spiritual revival"), as well as politics, the media, absolutely everything, is based on eradicating whatever is not Croatian. The implanting of the fundamental principles in the culture context was aided by nameless "volunteers": librarians, booksellers, bookstore owners, publishers, editors, officials at various cultural institutions, writers, journalists, university professors . . . The fundamental principles over these last thirty years have not changed. The only difference now is that the rule of adhering to these principles goes on behind the scenes, camouflaged. The policy of linguistic and cultural discrimination continues to stand firmly on nationalist and exclusivisitic foundations. This was recently confirmed (after thirty years of Croatian praxis!) by the kerfuffle when the Ministry of Culture refused to furnish Croatian libraries with copies of Serbian author Radomir Konstantinović's brilliant book *Filosofija palanke* [*The Philosophy of Parochialism*], claiming that they were only willing to furnish Croatian libraries with books published in the Croatian language.

And furthermore, as a writer, I too have experienced this sort of treatment. My books were also relegated to the waste bins. My readers may believe me or not, that's up to them. However, Ante Lešaje's 600-page book is a credible, and, I hope, trustworthy text. If they had even the tiniest shred of collective shame, the Ministry of Culture would publish a new edition of Lešaje's book and hand it out for free to all secondary schools, university departments, and libraries, as an apology for their appalling, continuing cultural libricide. I understand. There are no funds available for this because all the funds have already been spent on Tuđman's literary-historical "wasteland" and the monuments raised to him throughout Croatia which are, in every possible sense—from political to moral and ecological to aesthetic—an insult to the Croatian environment. And the Bosnian environment. Stupidity is, it seems, a force with imperial ambitions. Meanwhile, savvy Ireland has been repaying their debt to James Joyce by subsidizing the printing of his books, which sell for barely more than two euros. In short, Ireland has James Joyce, while Croatia has—Franjo Tuđman!

Somewhere you quote Radovan Karadžić as saying: "I am no monster, I am a writer." Indeed, should one perhaps leave a literature behind once it has been inhabited by Radovan Karadžić and others of his ilk?

I left all that behind nearly thirty years ago. I cannot understand how anyone can endorse Croatian literature yet fail to raise their voice in defense of their discriminated and suppressed colleagues, male and female, especially those colleagues who are Serbs. Moreover, there are those who have been pouring oil on the fire. How can anyone claim to be a Croatian writer who has failed to protest the rehabilitation of Ustasha writers such as Vinko Nikolić—with his lackluster literary ambitions and provincial skills—author of the *Ustaška književnost* [Ustasha Literature] manifesto? The post-1990 Croatian government adorned this returnee from South America with laurel wreaths. Ustasha education minister Mile Budak has been fully rehabilitated. During the Second World War he was the official responsible for implementing Nazi racist laws. Later, Slobodan P. Novak, a Croatian literary authority, proclaimed Budak the "Croatian Homer." During the 1940s, when the Independent State of Croatia was in power, this same Croatian Homer sent thousands of Jews, Serbs, and Romas to death camps. There are streets and even a few elementary schools named after him in Croatia. In Bosnia and Herzegovina, Mostar has a secondary school that bears his name. It is truly appalling, even nauseating, and, as far as I am concerned, morally impossible, to belong to a literature which embraces the national, literary, intellectual, and moral values of Ustasha writer Mile Budak. Could I, as a woman of Yugoslavia, who no longer has her country, accept a different sort of cultural concept? A Serbian one? Or Bosnian? Montenegrin? Macedonian? I cannot. All I could choose was to leave this cultural territory which was no longer mine anyway. I feel it morally insulting to belong to a literature where talent is measured by one's blood type. As far as female authors are concerned, even their blood type isn't enough. While we're on the subject of Homer, Ivana Brlić Mažuranić is the true Homer of Croatian literature. She towers over Croatian literature like a literary Himalaya, overshadowing many of the Croatian authors of great renown. I should add that Stanko Lasić, who came up with the Himalaya metaphor, was, as were many of his colleagues, obsessed by mighty male alpine imagery. Mount Triglav used to serve as the Yugoslav metaphor for the highest peak, but as it is now figures only as Slovenian, Stanko Lasić replaced it, in Croatian newspeak, with the more cosmopolitan concept of the "literary Himalaya." After Croatian independence, the notion of the "vertical" as the way of describing key figures of major cultural significance began appearing in Croatian self-flattering discourse, with phrases such as: "moral verticals," "colossi," "spiritual giants" ("Franjo Tuđman, the Croatian George Washington"), as well as the oft-used adjective, "esteemed." The most fashionable word at the moment is "great." The great so-and-so. As the *great* Petar Petrović Njegoš once said: *Among small nations the nest hides the geniuses* . . . Women are never described as verticals, especially not moral verticals. Indeed, men generally tend to think of women as horizontal.

I do hope that my question (Whence this unceasing thirty-year animosity from the official Croatian cultural community toward me?) won't come across as self-aggrandizing. When I quit my job at the Zagreb University School of Humanities and Social Sciences in 1993, when—by my own free will—I left my position, one of the professors, a tireless champion of European cultural values, asked me where I was going from there. When asked by a female colleague why he wanted to know, he said: "So as soon as possible we can warn everyone there about who is coming to work with them." Propaganda in the spirit of "guess who's coming to dinner" became the stock and trade of the resourceful members of Croatian PEN and the Society of Croatian Writers. After leaving Croatia I saw some of the letters Croatian cultural institutions sent to my translators and fellow Slavic scholars. Not to speak of my books, which, even when they were published, were nearly impossible to find on local bookstore shelves. Can I prove this? Unlikely. Can I prove the silence that dogged my books for years? Perhaps I could, but there could be a legitimate answer: reviewers and readers were not interested in them, which is, in part, true. The gist of a young writer and reviewer's comment about *Baba Yaga* was that it is boring because it is about little old ladies. A legitimate critical position, is it not? Were things any different in the old days when critics praised me? No. Whether praising or chiding, this was the same bourgeois Croatian environment, the same little provincial gossipy Zagreb, imagining itself a Vienna. Who scrambles for applause from such places? In politics that would be the father of the nation, Franjo Tuđman, and his cronies. The only artists who deign to fight for such applause are the Composer Foltins of the world—*Composer Foltin* being a work by Czech writer Karel Čapek.

And then I have a question for Croatian cultural authorities: What is it that is so specific about the Croatian cultural identity that I should hold it in higher regard than I do my Slovenian, Serbian, Bosnian, Montenegrin, North Macedonian, Bulgarian, Albanian, East-European, Russian, English, or American cultural identity? The burnings of books by authors who do not have a suitable ethnic identity? Blood type? The ethnic culture wars between the Croatian and Serbian communities? The literary arbitration of the incompetent, who are forever invoking their *fundamental principles*? The only upside for Croatia is its size. Croatia is a small country and such things are seen by very few outside of it. If the Serbs hadn't been the first to come up with the catchy tune "Whoever claims Serbia is small is lying," it could just as well have been the Croats. True, ridiculing the ambitions of others generally ends poorly for whoever dares to mock. So it should be said that Croatia is not entirely invisible. The war may have ended years ago but the Serbian side goes right on broadcasting its same tuneful message. And Croatia, responds, like in a musical: *It is not small, no not small, always ready for war, and will go again, will go again, never to be enslaved.*

Although this may seem a paradox, traditional discourse is livelier and more influential today than any other ideological expression of identification. The former Yugoslav concept of culture has now been left in the dust by what they refer to as traditional national culture. The language of that culture comes across through folk chants, silent circle dances, droning guslas and so forth, or historical fabrications such as popular medieval tournaments, which are meant to show that the Catholic Croats (Poles, Czechs, Lithuanians, Latvians, Estonians, etc.) have always been part of the European cultural zone, not the zone of Orthodox Communism. Take, for instance, the chivalric Alka games where men wearing impressive costumes use javelins to spear a symbolic "virgin," a wrought iron ring known as the *alka*. I have always thought of this performance—attended every summer by the entire Croatian political elite, just as the Yugoslav elite was there in days gone by—as a pornographic act. It is interesting that the numerous promoters of traditional culture have struck a note with the financial heart of the EU. The EU is guided by the principle of funding projects that bring together tourism and regional traditional culture. (Like their financial support of literary festivals!) Traditional culture is underwritten by the Ministry of Culture because this way it can flog empty platitudes about national identity. The Yugoslav praxis was similar in supporting national and ethnic identities through various forms of amateurism. In other words, we chanted, droned, danced, and strummed during Yugoslavia, too, cultivating and building brotherhood and unity. On we dance and strum, today, but supposedly we are no longer under pressure to dance and strum with those of other blood types.

What lies hidden behind the phenomenon of reliance on a collective identity?

Contemporary authors, who ought to be building cultural continuity, according to certain culture-based acceptable forms of behavior, or to build it up where it has been damaged, tend to do the opposite.

But perhaps also at fault are our cultural genes and memes, cautioning writers that little Croatian, Serbian, and the other kindred cultures defining their identity by blood type do not and cannot exist. Instead, there are cultural accidents. Krleža is a cultural accident. And Andrić is a cultural accident. And memes remind us that culture *does not flourish* in infertile soil, that one *cannot make a living in culture*—here today, gone tomorrow. In today, out tomorrow. Today you're part of the curriculum, tomorrow you're in the trash. Today you're a monument, tomorrow—a pile of rocks.

And this dynamic is determined not by the police, but by our colleagues, our moral verticals, guided by the principle: *the more things change, the more they stay the same.* And furthermore, it is easy to compare the Croatian literary surveys and textbooks of literary history printed during Yugoslavia with the ones that have come out since then. I believe that readers of Croatian surveys conducted during Yugoslavia will find many names that are now no longer in circulation. They have been erased. I hope someone will make the effort to document this farcical thirty-year history of exclusion and inclusion of authors in the corpus. I find it reminiscent of the Communist praxis of retouching photographs. Now you see it, now you don't! There have been attempts to tear down Vladimir Nazor and excise Vladan Desnica from the corpus. Croatian cultural authorities threw Nikola Tesla out until they cottoned on to the fact that, oops, Tesla is known all over the world and therefore has commercial value for tourism. Today the Tesla case in Croatia has been handily packaged with the phrase: "American and Croatian inventor of Serbian descent."

While we're on the subject of language, does it seem as if we in the former Yugo-countries perceive language as an ideological tool and vital national substance?

This is definitely the most comic and tragic part of the whole suicidal story. To carve up a language into four because there were suddenly four separate states is an incredible instance of political and cultural violence. (And the official languages of North Macedonia and Slovenia are, respectively, Macedonian and Slovenian, while Albanian is the official language of Kosovo.)

This violence was effectuated by cordons of ethnic police, institutions, schools, university departments, ministries of culture. Most of the writers have adapted to this ethnic concept of culture, and these who oppose the anti-intellectual praxis have been branded enemies of the people.

I know something about this praxis because I have been through quite a lot of it myself. The political will of others declared me to be a *Croatian*—and not a *Yugoslav*, writer. And when I protested publicly, they erased me from Croatian literature. The animosity, I should add, was mutual: I felt immense relief at removing myself from Croatian literature. And now imagine how difficult it has been for me as an author (labeled by my adopted literary community as Croatian) to have to explain that I consider the ethnic classification of citizens to belong to the realm of human rights, yet at the same time it can be a manifestation of state violence. I was, and still am, an author whose first and last name are a challenge to pronounce, who comes from a country that is a challenge to find on a map of the world. I was, and still am, an author who does not hide that she grew up in a country, Yugoslavia, that once existed, but no longer does. I was, and still am, an author who writes and speaks a "dragon" language, all in all a language that was one and has now branched into four: *Croatian, Bosnian, Serbian,* and *Montenegrin.* I was, and still am, an author who aspires, with these references, to inscribe herself into the map of world literature and who brazenly insists on being treated as a *transnational* or *post-national* writer. All this sounds like mission impossible.

The Declaration on the Common Language which was informally adopted in 2017 and signed by a group of writers from all over what was Yugoslavia (and which I, also, signed), was evaluated by the Croatian Academy of Science and Art as a "pointless, absurd, and futile initiative desiring to bring into question the right of the Croatian people to their own Croatian language, which is acknowledged and standardized as one of the official languages of the European Union." Croatian poet, diplomat, and academician Drago Štambuk gave a speech at the Croatian Academy in 2022 when welcoming new members, thereby demonstrating what the Croatian language ought to be and the values Croatian literature ought to be affirming . . .

> Standing before the precious jewel of the Croatian language and literacy, as before this, the most sacred altar of our Homeland, let us be smaller than a mustard seed. Only from something so small may a heavenly plant issue forth; let us submit it to the Homeland, and let us not forget our deserving forebears. What we never have enough of is blessings, more sorely needed than all other efforts. May the Almighty who knows our ascents and our frailties, our talents and omissions, strengthen us all so that with creative love, like our esteemed forebears, we preserve our eternal Croatia. Let us be her shining sword and her silver shield—her defense from ever-lurking uncertainties, and give us, oh God, a discerning heart to build much-needed harmony so that, as a people, we can kindly and reasonably guide our footsteps through earthly and cosmic temptations that stretch before us during these challenging times and before an ever more anxious humankind. I hereby vow in my own name and the names of the

newly elected members before us today that we will, as members of this worthy institution, give of the very best of ourselves for the glory and pride of our one and only Homeland.

In 2022, after thirty years had passed since the break-up of Yugoslavia began, after the proclamation of independence of the former Yugoslav republics of Slovenia, Croatia, and on . . . The Croato-Serbian or Serbo-Croatian language was officially fragmented into the Croatian, Serbian, Bosnian, and Montenegrin languages, the histories were fragmented, as were the cultures, cultural myths, truths (the lies began to mount as the countries were established), and so forth. I believe that Drago Štambuk, a medical doctor, poet, academician, and retired Croatian diplomat, like the entire Croatian cultural colony, grew up with the Smurfs (Štrumfovi, Les Schtroumpfs, De Smurfen), the small colony of blue, humanoid beings who live in a forest, in little dwellings that look a lot like mushrooms. The Smurfs are a fictional community created by Belgian illustrator Peyo (Pierre Culliford). Aside from the many things that divide, but also unite communities, the Smurfs do, of course, have their own language. The Smurf's village is divided into north and south neighborhoods, and each of them has its own take on the Smurf language. In the language of the northern Smurfs, there is an object called a "bottle smurfer," while in the language of the southern Smurfs that same object is a "smurf opener." This story is, purportedly, a parody of the language war (taalstrijd) between the French and Dutch communities living in Belgium. There have been doctorates and research conducted about the interesting world of the Smurfs. A French sociologist proclaimed the

Smurf community "totalitarian and rascist," while the Peyo studio dismissed this as "grotesque and frivolous." All in all, the Croatian, Bosnian, Serbian, and Montenegrin Smurfs are similarly inclined. They are the ones authorized for this job—the educators in elementary, secondary schools and institutions of higher learning, the ministries if culture, the important national institutions, the academies, the media, and the (male) writers. So where are the women writers?

A resistance movement?!

The decades of animosity toward the witches exhibit the most extreme example of radical, traditionalistic, negative modeling of women. The branding, discrediting, demonizing, and calling for a public burning of *disobedient* women artists and intellectuals. What have you concluded from this? Are you still in touch with your colleagues who went through the same attacks?

Although there are many women writers today, discriminatory patterns persist. And women themselves, our female colleagues, contribute to it. We mustn't forget this. I'm sorry to say that there never was much of a commonality among the Witches from Rio. It was there in principle but not in reality. I don't believe I have ever made the acquaintance of Jelena Lovrić, the journalist. After the media scandal, Vesna Kesić and I met once in Amsterdam. Earlier on I was only slightly acquainted with Slavenka Drakulić, but since the media-fabricated witches' Sabbath we have run into each other occasionally at literary gatherings abroad. I have known Rada Iveković since we were university students. We occasionally write to each other over email, and meet now and then when circumstances take me to Paris or her to Amsterdam. Fortunately, the pandemic, Zoom, and Skype have been renewing lapsed ties. I respect my colleagues and there isn't a single thing I can see that has stood or would stand in the way of our sense of community. Still, our general reluctance to articulate our case was, in my opinion, a major strategic oversight. One colleague described the case of the Croatian witches as something some clumsy journalists set in motion and then it spun out of control, roughly like a bit of scampish male mischief. Another colleague retreated from publicly condemning the case into which she'd been dragged through no fault of her own. Was I, too, at fault? I was. Absolutely. I should have said everything, not holding back the names of people, their gestures and actions. And I behaved, and continue to behave, like the polite little girl who does not violate the rules of decorum. This is as if after you've been raped you make coffee for your rapist and promise you won't tell a soul about the little incident. Today it's difficult to say, but I only know there was also silence after our female colleagues in Serbia, Slovenia, Bosnia went through similar experiences. And in all the communities of ex-Yugoslavia there was systematic per-secution of those who were labeled enemies of the regime, with women front and center. This should have been said more loudly and clearly, though I am not sure that even then we would have been heard at all. Because of this oversight, our case has been treated as an *incident*, and not as the systematic Croatian praxis of raising enemies in order to scare the people of Croatia. Our oversight hurt those discriminated against by the regime for the same reasons. Our case—later characterized as "the most dis-graceful moment of Croatian journalism"—overshadowed, in a way, all the other disgraceful cases of Croatian journalism. The Croatian authorities have been pretending not to see the swasti-kas on the public Croatian political and cultural landscape and keep referring to them as "incidents" or "regrettable incidents." The witches were yet another regrettable incident. And Aleksandra Zec's murder was also a regrettable incident, was it not? One incident after another—and step by step, inch by inch, we find ourselves where we are now.

After the case of the witches, the number of women has been on the rise who are protesting abortion, the pro-life Catholics, the young right-wing vloggers, influencers and regime groupies who twerk vigorously for the Croatian political authorities.

What was the thrust of the judgment you received for the *Witches from Rio* lawsuit against *Globus* magazine?

Our whole case, as was true of many others, took a wrong turn due to gullibility, to our naive faith in fair jurisprudence. Our attorney suggested that we test the viability of a newly adopted law that had been designed to shield those who were victimized by the mudslinging of the media. He decided to treat each of our cases individually. It is difficult today to know whether his strategy was wrong. In the end it turned out, judging by majority public opinion (and we know that the media shape public opinion), that each of us was actually sabotaging the freedom of speech by pressuring the blameless media to pay us damages. From Day One I found myself trapped. If I pulled out from the humiliating legal procedure, I thought, I'd be undercutting my colleagues and our attorney's enthusiasm. I won my case last of all, after a full 17 years. *Globus* never apologized, though the judgment had required them to do so. In place of an apology they published an interview with "Professor" Aleksandar Flaker in 2010. The first thing that jumps out at the reader is the title: "Dubravka Ugrešić wasn't driven away." This was *Globus*'s new "fuck you," directed solely at me this time. In the interview the professor, whose student I had been and with whom I had collaborated for many years on the project of *The Glossary of the Russian Avant-Garde*, mentions that he was no longer reading my books now that I'd "moved abroad," since I'd "deliberately abandoned the (Croatian) community." Furthermore, the professor remarked that he was "not prepared to accept my publicity stunt," or that while abroad I'd "begun to advertise myself as a dissident, an émigré." The professor, also the author of *Poetika osporavanja* [The Poetics of Contestation], a volume of literary scholarship, had resolutely turned his back on "contestation" as an artistic and political gesture, and instead embraced the "poetics of compliance" or perhaps, better said, the "poetics of sycophancy." But what was the point of protesting that I hadn't been driven away when my former Croatian community and I had already agreed that I hadn't been driven away? Perhaps making the point yet again that I "was not driven away" was necessary, not so much to save face as for them to mask the other side of this parting of ways. What happened, in fact, was that by leaving I was dismissing them; the Croatian community, like every other post-Yugoslav community, had become toxic. *Pure Croatian air* was no longer breathable.

In the interview the professor voices a preference for "literature from the 'hood," for "middling literature." This was a typical populist maneuver. The professor had enrolled in that unforgettable typology of intellectual compromisers so aptly described by Czesław Miłosz in *The Captive Mind*. And I can add that my case was not the first or the last indication of the professor's will to compromise both intellectually and morally.

All in all, the entire concept of defense the attorney came up with, regardless of the positive outcome, fell flat on its face, not only because *Globus* never apologized for its vainglorious attempt at investigative reporting. The law itself soon proved to be rife with controversy. It seems that the person who benefited most from it was Tomislav Merčep, a war criminal, who answered for his crimes only after immense legal pressure was exerted, though he was never sent to prison. Every time a negative article appeared in print about him and his infamous misdeeds during the war, Merčep would sue the press. Thanks to judges sympathetic to the regime, the media had to apologize to the war criminal and pay him vast compensation.

Our eye is often caught by newspaper articles about gangbangs, when a group of men rapes a woman. Judging by the media, gangbanging seems to be a popular sport among the people of India. Don't let the media fool you. The Japanese, perhaps less proactive, apparently prefer bukkake, a group ejaculation inspired by a (female) victim. On the other hand, it should be added that these Indians and Japanese bangers are no smarter than dolphins. Dolphins swim in gang formations and often go for bangs, in other words the group rape of a straying female. Having said that, I should say that dolphins are supposedly mentally superior to the average human being. And furthermore, octopuses have two hearts, while people, wouldn't you know it, have only one.

And finally, to answer your question. The thrust of the judgment against *Globus* in the case of the Croatian witches could read as follows: Croatian men, go for it, gang and gangbang. Enjoy your freedom. This is the freedom you fought for.

You end your collection of anti-political essays, *The Culture of Lies*, with sentences that are—in the broadest sense—prophetic for you and the coming generations of writers and artists: *I invested my own money in the purchase of my broom. I fly alone*. Right here on my desk sits my copy of *The Culture of Lies*, always open to that page to remind me of what matters most. Those sentences bring together the need for oneself as a safe space, the meanings of learning and articulation, and economic independence, as well as engagement. Where are the post-Yugoslav heirs of the *witches* today? What lies ahead?

A new generation of women writers has been coming forth and this is the very best thing that could possibly have happened. Everywhere in the Yugo-zone there are feminist portals, and excellent film and theater directors, actresses, visual artists, and especially young documentary filmmakers who are hard at work. As I'm no longer living in what we have come to call the region, I find it hard to keep track of all of them. For many young people, Croatia is no longer their domicile, and the same holds true for Serbia, Slovenia, Bosnia. Young people are experiencing life beyond national borders as a kind of mental detox. It seems as if young artists are more and more prepared to take their artistic destiny into their own hands instead of expecting that the state, no matter what it is like, will be their sponsor, mediator, and agent. I think young people have realized that the nation state pampers its artists, but in return demands their service, this way or that, whether they want to serve it or not. Either you remain integrated and wait for them to honor you with membership in the Croatian Academy of Science and Art, or you opt for risk and the advantages of that more tangible artistic freedom. The young feminists who continue to live and act in all communities of the Yugo-zone don't care much for the national context. These young people, mostly women, represent resistance to mainstream culture, and they communicate without restraint among themselves along the Ljubljana-Sarajevo-Skopje-Podgorica-Priština-Belgrade-Zagreb lines.[1]

We must not forget, however, that thirty years of nationalist educational indoctrination have raised generations of young people who won't identify the phrase "For the homeland—at the ready" as a Fascist greeting, who proudly sport Croatian Ustasha insignia, and genuflect to the Croatian "heroes" and "defenders." We must not forget the young women who speak out for banning abortion. We must not lose sight of the fact that there are young people in all the zones of ex-Yugoslavia who have grown up as nationalists, if not, already, neo-fascists. There needs to be something to fill the void. For these young people I feel infinite pity. And nausea. This is the same sort of pity and nausea I felt when I watched the anti-vaxxer protests in Zagreb and the demonstrators' blather about freedom. Whose?

---

1 This includes "rebel writers" and "rebel readers"; a new generation of teenagers who are growing up with books such as *Furam feminizam* [I'm Driving Feminism] by Maša Veličković and Lamija Begagić; with magazines such as *Književstvo*, *Bonamag.ba*, *lgbt.ba*, *Bookvica.net*, *Booksa.hr*, *Kuš (The Culture-Art Pantry)* magazine, *Čupava keleraba*, *Elektro-beton*, *Glif* (a portal for literature and culture), *Libela* (a portal for gender, sex and democracy), *Vox-Feminae*, and others.

How do you experience today's post-Yugoslav culture—and literature?

Post-Yugoslav culture is a controversial and problematic semantic field. If by that we are simply referring to the period following the break-up of Yugoslavia and formation of the successor states, your question would be an easier one to answer. Though, admittedly, not in detail, because for more accurate answers there needs to be research conducted into the measures and activities implemented by these cultural bureaucracies and the formation and impact of national (nationalistic) cultural systems. The cultural policies of these systems are all the same. They are based on "confiscation of memory" (to use the title of one of my earlier essays), or the implantation of new memories. All this is playing out with a simple imperative: Let's erase Yugoslavia, erase the Yugoslav ideological praxis, Yugoslav cultural history, and then let's establish our national praxis and our own history! In Croatia this has meant, concretely, a positive re-assessment of the Independent State of Croatia during the Second World War, the reclaiming of its four-year history, but also revival of its praxis (the insignia, flags, coat of arms, the name of the currency—the kuna, the language, the personalities and, in part, the ideology), in other words embracing the Independent State of Croatia in the Croatian historical continuity at the cost of throwing Yugoslavia out of that continuity, and then the rehabilitation and decriminalization of Croatian Fascist praxis during the Second World War and the stigmatization and criminalization of the Croatian anti-fascist movement during that war, under socialism, and during Yugoslavism between the years of 1945 and 1991. Also significant has been the revival of Catholicism as the fundamental ideological platform upon which Croatian identity rests. The institutionalization of the Croatian language as the official language of the Republic of Croatia is key, the Language Act, the politization of the influence and activities of the Croatian Academy of Science and Art and Matica Hrvatska. A similar process has been underway in Serbia, Montenegro, and in Bosnia and Herzegovina (where the situation is the most complex, and the Serbian, Croatian, and Bosnian ethnic identities have equal standing). Post-Yugoslav culture is based on ethnic and national divides. The posthumous smash-and-grab robbery of shared cultural property continues to this day. Peoples' rights are defined by blood type, by the nationality and ethnicity of the participants. Language is not always a trustworthy principle for differentiation, as the idea of Yugoslavia predates its more or less successful manifestations. There have been Croatian writers who have written in Italian or German, some have written in Hungarian, Croats would occasionally write in Serbian, and there have been Serbs who have written in Croatian, but the *blood and soil* ideology remains the relevant principle for forming and articulating the national literatures, which is, in my—albeit isolated—opinion, a disgrace. This meanwhile demonstrates that literature is ideologically the most rigid of the arts, both in terms of reception and message. Hence a theoretical reflection on post-Yugoslav literature could be particularly useful for understanding and defining current and future literary praxis.

As far as the contemporary praxis is concerned, it is capitalistic. Profit is increasingly important, the profit of the facilitators—cultural workers, publishers, distributors, managers and so forth. And profit, of course, implies political profit as well.

What is literary and women's transnationality? Your post-national position?

As far as my personal position is concerned, I have always been inspired by Virginia Woolf and her words, so often cited: "As a woman I have no country. As a woman I want no country. As a woman, my country is the whole world." To be fair, the ostracisim I experienced at my job at the School for Humanities and Social Sciences in Zagreb in the early years of the war, and later, and to this day, the media attacks, the fact that some colleagues declared me a witch and an enemy of the people while others made no effort to challenge them, as well as my departure from Croatia so many years ago, in 1993—all these things have radicalized my position.

Besides, I apparently realized early on, more intuitively than intellectually, that the national canon is not my cup of tea, especially because no matter how hard I try, I will never be a part of it. Women writers are seldom embraced by national canons (take the example of Marguerite Yourcenar). I also realized that I would refuse, loud and clear, to be included in the national Croatian, Serbian, or any other literary canon, because the literary canon is understood as a guaranteed plot in the national cemeteries, in the first row, front and center; the pomposity and intellectual arrogance, undeserved boasting of small, unimportant literatures ruled by the male writers fills me with protest and profound disgust as does every form of discrimination of the other. Once you sort all that out within yourself—more intuitively, as I said, than intellectually—a realm of freedom opens up before you that is worth fighting for. This is the realm of transnational, post-national literature, or international literature. I need to shift to freedom my own discriminated position as a woman writer who comes from a non-existent or barely existing country, who writes in a minor language that has been broken up into four languages which are, essentially, the same. My freedom means having the freedom to choose among literary traditions, it means moving freely from tradition to tradition, from narrative to narrative, without the obligation of belonging to any one of them or even adhering to them completely. Or moving into a second or third language, an experiment that women writers are perhaps more inclined to try. For example, Jhumpa Lahiri, a US female author of Indian descent, emigrated for a time (or perhaps forever) into the Italian language. This freedom implies non-belonging, literary dissidence, anti-canonic thinking, oppositional vision, disrespect for imposed literary conventions, genres, narratives, and so forth. "What is a country but a life sentence?" asks the young, Vietnamese-American writer Ocean Vuong. Whether I have succeeded in evading my life sentence remains to be seen.

But while we're on the subject of "Balkan" men and "Balkan" women, and wondering what women should do, then there is for now a single quiet, almost semi-illegal and unique literary realm where the dialogue between the sexes proceeds on an equal footing. This realm is, surprisingly, folklore, particularly oral erotic poetry—a realm that was banned for many years. The ban was not official censorship but rather a tacit arrangement. Only in 1974 was a part of Vuk Karadžić's archive published as *Osobite pjesme i poskočice* [Particular Poems and Songs for Dancing]. This limited academic edition (by the Serbian Academy for

Science and Art) was finally reissued later for the general public as *Crveni Ban* (*Red Ban*), a collection of oral erotic poetry. This was, I think, a discovery much like the global discovery of Bulgarian women's choral singing (though, understandably, with far less media reach). The Bulgarian concerts were often described by the media with the two words: cosmic and mysterious.

Balkan oral literature (Bulgarian, Macedonian, Greek, Serbian) ventures into the realm of the subversive, with a strong theme of women's hedonism, a rarity in European literature, and it has the powerful effect of humor and emancipation. In this sense the Bulgarian-Macedonian song "Sedna baba da večera" ["An old woman sits down to dine"] is unforgettable. The first evening she eats a partridge, the next night she eats two pigeons as well as a partridge, on the third she adds three fried chickens, on the fourth she adds four rams, on the fifth, five cows, on the sixth, six humped camels, and on the seventh she adds seven barrels of wine to her groaning board. And like all the previous evenings, the woman fails to eat her fill, but this seventh evening she does "get very drunk."

This song is reminiscent of nursery rhymes (like: *There was an old lady who swallowed a fly*), where everyday female life is hued with strangeness, absurdity, often cruelty, exaggeration, humor. (Marina Warner cracked this theme wide open, along with English writers like Angela Carter). All in all, young literary scholars who study post-communist literatures are faced with the challenge of resetting the newly imposed literary coordinates regarding history, literary concepts, and evaluating national literatures, and, of course, confrontation with the other young scholars who

espouse traditional national values. The shared language of Croats, Serbs, Bosnians, and Montenegrins has been split into four.
Because of the devastating break-up of Yugoslavia, no longer is
the literary community or a history of that community possible. Local literary coordinates have returned to the traditional
well-trodden praxis of national (patriarchal) literature. Only
through one's national literature is it possible to come to world
literature, or so the cultural conservatives and populists contend.

After a literary evening some twenty years ago in Budapest, an
older woman approached me and asked me to sign a copy of my
book. I asked for her name, and she said: Katlin Ladik. Katlin
Ladik was a movie actress and multimedia poet and performer
and I'd actually seen her on the stage for the first (and last) time
when I was a first-year comparative-literature student at the then
excellent Zagreb ITD Theater. I have never forgotten that evening
because I saw something that night that was unique, original, and
extraordinarily powerful. Later I saw Katlin Ladik in a Yugoslav
movie, and that was more or less that. Without much effort and
difficulty, Ladik built an international career. People recognized
her exceptional vocal range. She was compared to the global singing star, Peruvian Uma Sumac. And then Ladik quietly vanished
from the Yugoslav art scene. Her original performance concepts
had been excommunicated by nationalism. Ladik was a member
of the Hungarian national minority. She performed half-naked,
read poetry with her remarkable voice, and did visual experiments.
During our encounter in Budapest I learned that she had moved
away from Yugoslavia because Yugoslavia had moved away from
her. Forced to declare her Hungarian ethnicity, she settled in Budapest, took Hungarian citizenship, and continued writing songs,

though mostly in Hungarian. Katlin Ladik was erased from the Yugoslav cultural memory, as were so many other cultural figures. She had been locked up in a national, ethnic, and gender cage, and the new nationalist and patriarchal cultural bureaucracy clipped her wings. Katlin Ladik's fate after the break-up of Yugoslavia was shared by many. Most of them adapted to the provincializing of culture which came with the collapse of (socialist) Yugoslavia, and a smaller number of them left the country that no longer existed anyway. Not to speak of the fact that Ivo Andrić, the only Yugoslav ever to be awarded the Nobel Prize for Literature, had his Yugoslav identity as a writer disputed and usurped as well.

The Culture of (self)harm

How to write and create as a woman in a culture that treats her as its enemy?

Classicist Mary Beard has written on the theme of discrimination against a woman's public voice in her article "The Public Voice of Women" (and in the book *Women & Power—A Manifesto*), where she offers examples which, I confess, I have quoted in my essay "The Scold's Bridle," published in *The Age of Skin*. Mary Beard mentions Lucretia, who was permitted to accuse her rapist publicly, but only if her suicide immediately followed her denunciation. Also here is the story of Philomela, whose tongue was cut off by her rapist to prevent her from testifying against him, the story of Io, transformed by Jupiter into a cow, thereby stripping her of her right to speech, left only able to moo. (By the way, in Russian modern slang, *tyolka*, or little calf, is a slang word for girl, the equivalent of the English word *chick*!). Hera behaved similarly when, out of jealousy, she condemned Echo to give voice only to the words of others.

Beard also offers a detail about Penelope who cheerfully challenged her son Telemachus. He responded fiercely (more or less) like this:

"Mother, go back up into your quarters. Tend to your own tasks, the loom and the distaff . . . Speech will be the business of men, and me most of all: I hold the reins of power in this house."

Here I recall again my colleagues who so cheerfully urged me to stick to my sewing machine, referring to my short novel, *Steffie Cvek in the Jaws of Life*. Their message was, essentially, that I should "shut my mouth," "because speech is the business of men." Another colleague coined the phrase "kitchen literature," which implies that women can only produce trivial writing, and the kitchen, aside from the bathroom, is the most trivial part of the house. This is roughly as if I were to dub men's writing "bordello literature" because the bordello is the only place where male authors experience flights of universal imagination, missing at the ground-level and in grounded kitchen literature. The pattern, hence, is ancient. This is a culture of systematically stripping away one's right to speech, and the victims are most often women. And slaves.

For centuries women have been denied their right to articulate their knowledge, skill, and critical thinking. What does culture in all its glory have to tell us?

Maybe this is the real answer to the question of why there are so few women in literature, and why they have been missing for so long. Women's emancipation generally arrives too late. When Cicero was put to death and his head was displayed in the Forum, Fulvia, Mark Anthony's wife, who had often been the target of Cicero's ridicule, came to see it. Legend has it that

Fulvia plucked a hairpin from her hair and with it she stabbed Cicero's tongue.

Men's hatred for women has always zeroed in on language (*That dame has a tongue like the tail on a cow!*), on women's big mouths, on women "shutting" their mouth, on denying women's right to speech, on a systematic refusal to engage in dialogue with women, on the men's insatiable need to dominate. Denial of the right to speech has been shown to be more efficient than the taking of a life. Scheherazade was the first woman who fought for her right to speak in the high-risk profession of female author. She defended her right by laying her head on the chopping block one thousand and one times.

The *scold's bridle* or *witch's bridle*, a muzzle for chatterboxes, was fastened—often at the request of a woman's husband or members of her family— over a woman's face, over her tongue and mouth, in the sixteenth and seventeenth century in England, Scotland, and the British colonies. Shakespeare explores the theme of communication between the sexes in his comedy *The Taming of the Shrew*, where the woman is permitted to speak, but only in a way that suits the man, in a voice that is sweet, soft, meek. The key word here is not harming but taming, which is closer to the next example, the popular play *Pygmalion* by George Bernard Shaw. Shaw camouflages the inflexible stereotype of the man in an atypical male figure, Henry Higgins, a professor of phonetics. Higgins would like to transform a London flower seller into a lady but she speaks in thick cockney. How? By teaching her to speak proper English. And when he brings the flower seller up to his linguistic, aesthetic, and class standards, Higgins falls in love with her. G. B.

Shaw's play is a version of the myth about Greek sculptor Pygmalion who falls in love with his own sculpture, Galatea.

How do you see current aesthetic-culturological praxis in terms of the historical?

Men persist, unrepentant, in adapting women to their own aesthetic standards. A vast cosmetic industry has developed in response to men's Pygmalionesque fantasies, perhaps one of the most profitable industries in the world, and plastic surgery is one of the most heavily subscribed branches of surgery. Every year surgeons correct millions of noses, breasts, buttocks, mouths, teeth, they use liposuction to suck fat away, and they remove women's ribs to give them a slimmer waist. Standards change. One year the aesthetic fetish is all about noses, the next year it's breasts, in the third it's the mouth, in the fourth—the buttocks. Millions of women the world over are dolls in somebody's hands, though they are convinced that they themselves are in control and that their body is their freedom. Women have become a mighty army of dolls who come marching out of the factories for doll manufacture and repair. And all of them, naturally, look alike. The difference among them used to be skin color, when Barbies were only white, but then the industry caught on and realized that political correctness could be profitable, all the more so because wealth is no longer the privilege of the colonizers, the whites, but is gradually becoming the privilege of the decolonized as well. One of the women, who went through numerous cosmetic operations until she transformed herself into a living Barbie, confessed: "Plastic surgery has been my key to a better life."

But physical beauty in the life of a woman has always played a major role . . .

No, a woman's beauty has always played a major role in the life of men. Men bought beauty. Many are shocked by the information that for centuries in China there was a cosmetic procedure known as *foot-binding*, the custom of wrapping the feet of select young girls until their feet turned into little hooves, or, in Chinese imagology, into the golden lotus blossom. This is how wealthy men turned their wives into crippled beauties who were no longer able to walk, who were imprisoned in their homes, who were living dolls in the hands of their guardians. Yet it's also true that her bound feet dramatically changed the woman's social status.

One oughtn't, however, rush to random conclusions based on random knowledge. When someone in Austria showed me a graphic portrayal of Langtüttin, the Tyrolian folklore witch, I was reminded of the Chinese victims of foot-binding. In old photographs, the Chinese beauties look like goddesses, their faces mysterious and their demeanor befitting a ruler—not a victim of physical violence. Langtüttin, the female folklore demon, has long pendulous breasts that she slings, scarf-like, around her neck. She poisons children with black milk, while on her legs, instead of feet, she has tiny hooves that look a little like the deformed feet of the Chinese beauties. According to imagology, mythic beings are revealed by a detail, a physical anomaly, which distinguishes them from ordinary people, an ambivalence, invalidity (a single eye, for instance, instead of two), a more or less visible mark that signals plausible transhuman identity. Mythic beings are set apart from ordinary people primarily by their capacity for metamorphosis, transformation. All this fantastical world has moved into the entertaining media, to comic books, video games, movies, television series about vampires, morphs, werewolves, witches, beings with superpowers. True, the move from dusty books into the gleaming visual media environment seems like going from a library to a circus. But this circus insures visibility, longevity, some sort of cultural continuity, and, of course, profit.

I would like someone to explain the difference between foot-binding and the plastic surgery procedures such as liposuction, buttock enhancement, breast augmentation or reduction, and lip enhancement. When analyzing contemporary social codes, strategies, coordinates, fashion, and customs there is no need to moralize but instead to rely on factual, historical, as well as mythical, cultural patterns. Will hugely enhanced lips turn an ordinary young woman into a mythical being? The media made a fuss over the single remaining Chinese woman who had undergone foot-binding, just as today they follow the transformations of some young women who have had minute tattoos done on their eyeballs. What is the difference between these experiments and foot-binding? What is the difference between eyeball tattoos and clitorectomy? Is the first an individual choice while the other is an act of violence?

What do popular fairy tales or other works of art have to tell us?

There are countless examples. But at the moment I am thinking of Lars von Trier and his early movie, *Breaking the Waves* (1966).

The story was about a god-fearing woman whose beloved husband has an accident at work and is thereafter confined to his bed. The man asks his wife to have sex with other men and then tell him about her experiences, as this is the only thing that will keep him alive. The woman does what he asks and then does so more and more often, until in the end she goes off on a ship and allows herself to be raped by a dozen sailors. The woman is dying in the belief that her sacrifice will heal her husband. And, so it is, her husband regains his mobility! I remember really liking the movie when I first saw it. Today, a quarter of a century later, I think Trier's movie is a variety of religious moralist pornography that unmasks the perverse essence of male-female relations—physical, mental, and moral mutilation.

On the other hand, Andersen's Little Mermaid saves a winsome prince from death, and then agrees to self-harm. She trades her divine voice for a pair of shapely women's legs, gives up her watery identity, as well as the powers that this identity brings with it. And she does all this to capture the prince's heart. Yet the prince doesn't recognize the Little Mermaid as the woman who saves him from certain death and off he goes to marry someone else.

There are, of course, countless other examples. The format of this conversation, however, does not allow us to explore them in greater depth. I apologize for that here both to you and to the readers who may be expecting more expertise in my responses and less sloppiness. Though intellectual sloppiness does have its upsides. In *Threepenny Opera,* Bertold Brecht says: The chief thing is to learn to think bluntly. Blunt thinking is great thinking.[2] I rely

---

2 Die Hauptsache ist, plump denken lernen. Plumpes Denken, das ist das Denken der Großen.

immodestly on these words, which serve me as a sort of alibi or auto-ironic excuse.

Aside from instructing little girls, we, too, practice desirable models of self-harm. Why? Are we lacking true feminist strategies of emancipation?

The extraordinary popularity of Frida Kahlo says something about this. She was resurrected like a female Jesus on the cross thanks to feminist readings of the history of women's creativity. Countless biographies, monographs, and fictionalized biographies have come out about Frida Kahlo. She has become a cult, a symbolic figure who best represents the historical pattern of the mutilation and (self)harming of women. Kahlo is now an identification point for female trauma. She is an invalid, she falls in love with her much older mentor, Diego Rivera, then marries him and lives in his shadow. Many women have found a similar focal point for identification in the persona of Sylvia Plath. In their effort to construct a pattern that would represent male–female relations, feminists have reached for male strategies of instrumentalizing women's destinies. Today I think that this feminist strategy, if that is what is going on, is missing key emancipational potential.

Can you explain this? What do you mean by "emancipational potential"?

I don't know if you've noticed that within the broadly understood realm of culture the dominant pattern of woman-victim has not changed. Women are victims of sexual violence, family relations, victims of a violent father, a submissive mother, a war, economic and financial constellations, they are victims of illness, dependency, alcoholism, mental illness, bulimia, anorexia, self-harm, lookism (imposed standards of beauty), gender discrimination, professional discrimination, they are victims of imposed gender roles and functions (giving birth, motherhood, sexuality), and all manner of other things. I am a witness to the growth—a boom—and, ultimately, the commercialization of vital "women's themes" over the last fifty-odd years. There have been advances of inestimable value: the opening, diagnosing, and researching of women's themes, the tearing down of taboos related to women's themes, the popularization of women's themes (from the globally popular Oprah Winfrey to the women working on feminist theory), historical research, anthropological research, as well as the systematic "feminization" of various spheres of human activity in politics, art, science, scholarship, education, and so forth. Film, the visual arts, literature, these disciplines have also been feminized. Gender studies, women's institutions, literary, television, cinematic genres that have been enriched thanks to women's participation (memoirs, confessions, autobiographies, speculative literature, popular culture), philosophy, colonial studies, the living praxis of cultural decolonization and emancipation. All these positive changes have happened in an astonishingly short time.

And yet, the existing conglomeration of cultural products would seem to suggest that the woman is still the victim. The woman-victim dominates as the cultural archetype. Every ten years or so, a new generation of women rises and takes on the struggle for the same cause, wielding the same weapons, while scarcely knowing anything about who the women are who have come before. Women seem forever to be sabotaging themselves, scoring own-goals over and over again. I cannot understand this and I cannot explain why it happens. Is the force of inertia insurmountable? If so, has the time come for us to make our peace with this? The global bestsellers, largely purchased by women, are the best indicator of the force of inertia. One such global bestseller, *Fifty Shades of Grey*, appeared ten years ago from the workshop of British female author E. L. James. This book, or rather trilogy, has been translated into fifty-two languages and has sold millions of copies, not to mention the enormous popularity of the derivatives—the movie version of the novel and the production of the sado-masochistic toys that are described in the novel.

After everything that has happened it does seem as if the archetype of woman-victim wins, just as, after all the "battles," there is always a comforting cultural archetype for humankind (for one part of humankind, of course)—Jesus Christ. Porno stars, pop singers, actresses, various Oprah Winfreys, female authors, female artists, female influencers—all of them, like most women, identify as a matter of principle with the woman-victim archetype. We all need the "biblical" stories of martyrdom, the story, the passage through humiliation (rape, sexual molestation, subservience, confession, and the final absolution from sin), so that at the end of her martyrdom the woman has the right to reincarnation. Without a passage through this religious rite there can be no enlightenment. Women must bear the "cross" on their backs, acquiesce to clichéd confessions in order to pretend to "saintly" status (from sinner to saint!). Frida Kahlo's self-portrait ("Frida Kahlo & Diego Rivera: A Love Revolution") with a small portrait of Diego Rivera imprinted on Frida's forehead is a fundamental message that almost all women can identify with.

Stewardess-martyrs working for almost all the airlines negotiate the narrow aisle in high-heels and tight skirts, though it would be healthier for them and for the passengers if they were wearing soft tennis shoes and comfortable pants. As a passenger I always wonder how I can possibly expect help from someone who is wearing high heels on an airplane that may dip and lurch. By the same token why don't stewards walk around with their buttocks bare? Perhaps that would soothe my jittery travel nerves. Not only mine, but the jitters of those passengers with homosexual inclinations. And the world, not only at the higher altitudes but on the ground, is full of similar details, signaling that the world finds changing difficult. We are capable of inventing swifter aircraft, but the stewardesses will go right on wearing tight skirts and high heels.

The Virgin Mary, Frida Kahlo, pop singers, female artists, female authors of memoirs, autobiographies, fiction and faction, many women, including Croatian mega pop star Severina— are icons, women models, model women. They have all been through the same religious process, which the broader public recognizes and with which, thanks to the religious gene, they can easily identify. Marina Abramović, for example, has finally been recognized as a great world artist, but only after *The Artist is Present*, the three-month long performance she engaged in at MoMA in 2010. For a full three months, Abramović sat, dressed in robes reminiscent of the Virgin Mary's clothing, and stared in silence at her "faithful followers." The gallery-goers were deeply moved by this scene of artistic-religious "self-sacrifice." Sometimes the Virgin Mary let a tear slip out, sometimes several tears when bidding farewell to Ulay, her former artistic and life partner. If a resurrection is to take place, there needs to be more than just the story about humiliation, sacrifice, self-sacrifice, forgiveness. There should also be witnesses, recorders (writers of hagiographies and hagiographic versions), students, admirers, followers, or, as in recent usage, fan bases. Even Jesus Christ couldn't have had a more finely attuned promotional strategy. This archetype is also imprinted on our civilization's collective memory, like a permanent tattoo.

Yes, but doesn't the lack of "emancipatory potential" influence the value of a literary work? We know there was a period of socialist realism where works had to celebrate labor, productivity, optimism, and Soviet rule. Should we start a trend for socialist-feminist realism?

I believe there is something else going on here, or so it seems to me. Religious genes are implanted in all of us, regardless of our personal religious affiliation or absence thereof. If we aren't devout, this does not mean that our religious gene won't kick in sooner or later, even without our will and awareness. Croats have their internationally celebrated healer, Braco (*Braco's Gaze*), who does nothing but stand for a long time on stage, gazing soulfully at his sizeable, deeply moved audience. Braco is difficult to categorize in terms of gender and age, which only augments, of course, his popularity. With his vulnerable appearance and long-ish hair, he looks like a fifty-year old adolescent who has peed in his pants and now, wracked by guilt, gazes into the crowd of people, seeking their forgiveness for the unfortunate accident. Religious and political tricksters with a nose for the media (and what other kind of tricksters are there?) know where our acupuncture points are. Vladimir Nabokov said somewhere that the success of a book needn't be attributed to its author but to the readership, hence, the majority Sacred Consumer. And our buddy Braco knows all about this.

It would seem that there is more gender emancipatory potential in a low-budget television series like *Buffy the Vampire Slayer* (about a teenager battling vampires), than in the much-touted products of commercialized feminism. One needn't forget, however, that all these orientations are controlled, directed, and homogenized and then gradually erased—by the mighty market. Currently I have the impression that the entire creative industry has shifted its focus to youth. Hence the remarkable popularity of television series featuring teenagers, of young adult literature, and of the youthful or rejuvenated cultural industry. Slowly but surely, adults are being pushed to the margins. Ours is a cult of debutantes, of the hyperproduction of workshops for creative writing and all other forms of "artistic" expression, the fast-tracked training of young creative talents in the industry, and so forth. Everyone is making money off of everyone else. One of the potential outcomes is the drastic infantilization of global culture, including literature. This infantilization even has an impact on some of the heavy-weight intellectual disciplines such as philosophy. Well-trained philosophers popularize their knowledge by adapting it to the "uninformed" reader, and as far as the genre itself is concerned, translating it into a sort of self-help literature. True, I am aware that my assertion regarding widespread infantilization requires greater depth; stated so baldly it comes across as little more than an ugly generalization. For if ideas, too, are a product subject to the laws of the market, we must take into account many market aspects including the price of this product and its popularity. Age limits have been abolished and young authors, particularly female authors, are increasingly successful, thanks to the mechanisms of the market, at imposing their vision of the world and their values, whether their vision of the world is *authentic, groundbreaking, emancipatory*, or not. But, how to determine what is *authentic, groundbreaking, emancipatory*? Compared to what? Can *authentic, groundbreaking, emancipatory* have any relevant value for literature and art of the digital age when everything can simply be copied? And besides, hasn't a child, Mark Zuckerberg, subjugated and enslaved us all? Zuckerberg has changed our global awareness and conscience to his exclusive (material) benefit and our detriment. This all depends, of course, on the way one looks at it. Zuckerberg seems to me like a child who has turned the world into a global gossip mill and holds the monopoly.

And as far as market mechanisms and promotional models are concerned, they are most simply explained by celebrated (and highly commercial) violinist Joshua Bell, who acquiesced to an experiment recorded by a hidden camera. Bell, one of our modern "musical saints," camouflaged as a street musician, played the violin for forty-five minutes at one of the subway stations in Washington DC. A total of 1,097 passengers walked by Joshua Bell, the "beggar," during his forty-five-minute performance. Only seven of them stopped briefly to listen, and only one of them recognized him. Joshua Bell earned $32.17 for his masterful performance. Twenty-seven passersby tossed money into his hat. The person who recognized him boosted his take by tossing in a $20.

It seems to me that we are always forgetting the fact that the self-harm of women has its most powerful support in religion.

Religion is absolutely the most durable, brutal, and forceful harmer of women and women's self-confidence. This refers mainly to the powerful monotheistic religious systems—Judaism, Christianity, and Islam—which cover the most territory on the global map of religions, including more than 50% of the faithful on planet Earth. The Church has radically harmed women, introducing a strict bureaucratic hierarchy, while brutally harming the more emancipated women's pre-Christian imagination and adapting it to its misogynistic religious concept. The pre-Christian world was ruled by a more democratic polytheism, mighty gods and goddesses, demi-gods, the offspring of promiscuous relationships between ordinary people and the gods. In the authoritarian religious systems, instead, a single (male) god rules and creates people in (his) image. His offspring never question the credibility of God, because should they dare to do so, they would be met with the most terrible of all punishments, their father's, a divine punishment. God fashioned Adam's companion Eve from Adam's rib, thereby permanently defining her position as inferior, dependent on Adam. This biblical tale is also one of the most perverse products of the human imagination. All in all, my hypothetical dad is Adam, my hypothetical mom is Eve, who was made from my dad's rib. As brainpower is clearly not Adam's strong suit, he obediently heeds Eve's desire to taste the apple from the forbidden tree of wisdom. And then, presto, both of them are punished by being banished from paradise, and, what's more, Eve is forever to blame, because she was the one who pushed Adam into this culinary adventure. Ever since then the Church has had it in for Eve. For her every intellectual urge, Eve has been symbolically or actually punished—from her banishment out of Eden to this day. Witches were burned at the stake from the twelfth to the seventeenth centuries in Europe. The Church has never felt moved to apologize for the systematic murder of women, for the massive carnage it has committed, for their femicide, unparalleled in world history. Of course femicide is not only a religious historical and symbolic specialty. Every year approximately 800,000 people are victims of one of the fastest growing businesses in the world ($32 billion dollars annually)—human trafficking. Eighty percent of the victims are women, of whom more than 50% are not yet adults. Have the state institutions (and the Church) found a way to stop this form of femicide? It still doesn't occur to god-fearing Adam to blame his "father" for all these crimes. Adam continues to vent his frustrations on Eve. The supposed 7% of atheists the world over cannot disperse this intoxicating, self-satisfying, authoritarian fog of religion all by themselves. The institution of religion—which is certainly the most enduring autocratic system we know—has been going on for two millennia, but, surprisingly, very few seem to think of it as autocratic.

What should women do?

The theme we have touched on is simply indomitable. Women all over the world are fighting with a wide assortment of "weapons" on many fronts, doing what they can to examine and articulate aspects of the centuries of humiliation of women. It is important to know that the gender question is perhaps one of the most complex issues facing civilization and society; everything is interwoven with it. This is something feminist theorists, fighters for women's rights and activists, have known for a long time, which is why they call for an intersectional approach. Everything is profoundly interconnected, the women's question, religious systems, class relations, customs, biology, psychology, sexuality, history . . . My conversation with you confirms that all aspects of this vast theme are simply impossible to encompass in a systematic way. There is an endless amount of professional literature confirming that we need gender studies as acutely as we need oxygen. Here we are merely scratching the surface. All of us women scholars, philosophers, writers, anthropologists, sociologists, activists are working on amassing knowledge in a vast library, which gradually or radically, quickly or slowly, is shifting the general perspective. All in all, I cannot tell women what to do. What matters most, I think, is for them to claim, or succeed in retaining and expanding, their right to a public voice, which woman has been denied by male will: entirely, partially, by law or by custom.

The word "mansplaining" has been circulating widely, designating a strategy of sabotage, disparagement, interruption, silencing, and patronizing of female speakers by men. In societies where women have won their right to public speech, there are still strategies being shamelessly employed to sabotage women's speech in the media, on television, in the newspapers, in public discourse where the male participants override, interrupt, and disparage their female interlocutors or simply refuse to enter into a dialogue with them.

To learn the real meaning of the modern term "mansplaining" we should all read "Zlostavljanje" ["Maltreatment"], a short story by Ivo Andrić. Men and women readers will learn everything they need to know about mansplaining in it. Andrić's brilliant analysis of men's misogyny, stemming from a profound male complex of inferiority, has not been outshone, even across the larger terrain of world literature. Every ministry of culture— Slovenian, Croatian, Bosnian, Serbian, North Macedonian, Montenegrin, Albanian—should print up Andrić's story and distribute it for free, as they do vaccinations. The mainstream "Balkan man"—whether he be politician, worker, writer, official, professor, soccer player, intellectual, or criminal—is captured in the description of boss Andrija Zekerović, Andrić's abuser. Every "Balkan woman," should she want to, can recognize in the character of Andrija the politicians of her mini-state, her husband, her lover, her brother, her own son, a friend, a neighbor, as well as contemporary authors whose books, don't you know it, continue to be read with undiminished satisfaction.

Map to Map—Mapping

In what way can we de-canonize (national) literary and culturo-logical canons?

It is impossible to accomplish anything positive without earlier fundamental social changes. The Republic of Croatia is founded on a lie. These foundations have been reinforced for a full thirty years now. Imagine how many years it would take to undo the lies and start again from scratch. The lie is not just the hood-winking of a majority of voters, but it also serves as their alibi. (They lied to us! This is not our fault—we trusted them.) Regimes like the regime in Croatia have always been lacking in robust political activism, and we'll see what the social movements will be able to accomplish with the political parties that have recently formed in Croatia. There are many admirable activist initiatives throughout the Yugo-zone. The most enduring one, the Belgrade women's anti-war group *Women in Black*, is still active today with an unflagging persistence.

What is lacking in all the post-Yugoslav states is a culture of (left-ist) rebellion. This sort of culture is difficult to establish. Croatia has a mafia-like state structure, posturing to others as a war victim, though the war was thirty years ago. And Serbia does the same. This production of political caterwauling (the Croats are victims of Communism, victims of Serbian aggression, victims of the corruption of political elites) is unbearable. And meanwhile, at least from the outside, Croatia appears to be a spawning ground for a fresh generation of European fascists who have been issued the paperwork for legal political undertakings.

I would like to know what has happened to the Croatian "intellectuals" who served Milan Bandić, Zagreb's criminal mayor, with such an earnest devotion. Bandić ruled Zagreb and pillaged it for a full twenty years, and as mayor he purchased the support of the Croatian intelligentsia by granting them apartments, giving them jobs in cultural institutions and ownership of cultural venues in the city center. When journalists discovered that one of the people who'd been given one of the city's free apartments was a professor of literature—someone who served on committees, worked as an editor, authored several commissioned monographs, espoused the notion that mathematics has a national identity ("Croatian mathematics")—the mayor pulled off an impressive tear-jerking skit for the assembled journalists: "Bypassing the waiting list to grant apartments to deserving members of the community is up to the mayor's discretion. You have ruined my day, I will be sad now all day. Why do this? Dragging through the mud people who are the intellectuals and precious pearls of this country? I am sad. I really feel like crying. Do you know how much this man has done for this city and this country!?" This very same "precious pearl" of the Croatian state, who had nearly brought the mayor to tears, was the very man who initiated the media persecution of the Croatian witches, the former president of Croatian PEN, currently a retired professor of Croatian literature and a frequent guest on rightwing, neo-Ustasha television programs. It's a shame that there are no leftwing television programs, because this pragmatic "precious pearl of the Croatian state" would frequent both.

Whatever happened to the teams of Croatian intellectuals who have served for these last thirty years and continue to serve in the various ministries of culture, including the notorious, now former, minister of culture, popularly known by his nickname "Herr Otto Flick" (after a Nazi character—a Gestapo officer—from the British sitcom *'Allo 'Allo!*), who announced that he would pour all the money allocated for culture into building a monumental military museum? Did anyone make a fuss to stand up to him, or make even the smallest effort one can make in such situations, such as, for instance, resigning? There can be no forward movement (nor any de-canonization) without beefing up the culture of defiance. In Croatia the activities of the dominant rightwing and even righter rightwing are well known. So where is the leftwing opposition? It has dwindled in Croatia to a negligible handful of people. This situation, unfortunately, is no more optimistic in the other cultural environments in the "region" (ha, how easily what used to be a country can be reduced to a region!).

Here I should say that readers may see me as overstepping the bounds of fair play: I'm naming some people while not naming others. In principle I try to avoid naming names, because then the reader's attention is automatically drawn to the person, to the tree, in other words, rather than to the forest. The names are not crucial. The ones who matter are the numerous, active "nameless" participants, the willing. The willing executioners. Daniel Jonah Goldhagen has written about this phenomenon of collective participation his book *Hitler's Willing Executioners.*

Numbers are important when exposing lies. The more precise the figures, the better. I would love, for instance, for someone to tell me how much Croatia has increased the size of its police force since independence. During Yugoslavia there were, allegedly, 4,000 police officers. Today the police force, in Croatia alone, allegedly numbers 40,000. And this number, allegedly, continues to grow. Do these impressive numbers qualify Croatia as a police state, and, consequently, imply that the inhabitants of Croatia must be thieves and criminals? Meanwhile, as the number of police officers grows, the number of Croats is dwindling. This last statement has been confirmed by demographic data. There are more Croats abroad than there are in Croatia. How many soldiers are there in Croatia? Are the taxpayers footing this bill? How much is it? Germans were known to have handled the problem of unemployment in the former GDR (after the two Germanies united) by employing the young unemployed men, formerly East Germans, as soldiers. Is Croatia, in fact, a militaristic European enclave, the only purpose of which is to push back from the Croatian, i.e., EU, borders the many people who are on the move? And while we're on the subject of culture, here is a question: How many Catholic priests are there in Croatia and how much do they cost? We learn from the newspaper that each Croatian hospital has been required by law to employ at least one priest. The excessive production of priests (much like all those managers holding MBAs) has resulted in an inflation of the priestly vocation on the labor market. If the Croatian government persists with this policy we can expect to be greeted at car repair workshops by priests with wrenches in hand, while Croatian mechanics are cheerfully repairing Irish, German, and Swedish cars abroad.

We are living in a rightwing dictatorship. Call it what you like—a neo-fascist dictatorship, a populist dictatorship, or a democratorship (Predrag Matevejević coined the term "demokratura" from "diktatura." In English, "democratorship" has been coined from "dictatorship" by the same logic). All of us know what this is about. Some democratorships sprouted in the EU zone like poison mushrooms after a democratic rain. Croats have a depressingly weak-kneed, lackluster opposition intelligentsia. Because the majority intelligentsia in Croatia—as confirmed by the last thirty "democratic" years—is subservient, corruptible, and corrupted, they only dare to raise their voices when there is absolutely no risk involved that they will bear any consequences for what they say. The mantras about how culture mustn't be politicized come only from the ranks on the right. Those on the right allow themselves to politicize culture, moreover they are actively involved in precisely that. Only the minority, the left-oriented intelligentsia, is banned from doing so.

You asked how one might de-canonize national literary and political canons. First and foremost this requires what I'll call a gender-oriented enthusiasm. The reading, for example, of national canonic writers from a woman's perspective. Here is an amusing example. When writer Dobrica Ćosić became president of what was referred to as rump Yugoslavia—comprised of only Montenegro and Serbia—and when he went around saying: *I am here to serve you,* as if he were a headwaiter and not a writer, he provoked the animosity of a portion of the Belgrade reading public. Whenever they happened upon one of his books on their own shelves or in others' libraries, the anonymous demonstrators sent it to Ćosić's home address. The postal workers apparently had their hands full. Hundreds and hundreds of packages, or so goes the urban legend, piled up by the door of the literary "godfather," of this deserving Serbian classic.

What is your (women's) perspective on the dynamics of the condition of exile?

Try to imagine a trip you are embarking on, but you don't know whether you'll ever return and how long you'll be on the road; you aren't entirely sure why you are taking this trip, you don't ask too many questions, there must have been a good reason. And besides, if fear and restlessness arise, you find consolation in the thought that you can always buy a ticket and return *home.* The only thing you are bringing with you is a dictionary of foreign languages. Suddenly you discover that this dictionary is something magical. It divulges words whose meaning you weren't even searching for, like, bingo, the prefix "trans-." You wonder why, these are things you already know well—*trans-, across, over, beyond*—but you still don't understand. Then you notice that the words no longer seem to have the same meaning. This is where the confusion begins, words come flying out of the dictionary like flapping birds . . . Oh yes, the colors of the landscape around you are shifting, everything is suddenly different.

This may sound psychedelic, but it is the way you perceive things at first in exile, regardless of whether you have or haven't traveled before. Exile is a sort of contemplative snare, where your old convictions melt away, the stereotypes you grew up with and absorbed are deconstructed. Suddenly you measure, weigh, calibrate, what was before, what is now, and whether this "now" of yours has been your free choice or was coerced. The meaning of the concepts we have grown up with gradually shifts—*home, country, family, friendship, love, language, morals, education, history, identity, myself* . . . Concepts peel off of us like scabs from healing wounds. And the "magical" thing, the dictionary, continues to unsettle us. Exile is a process, and until the moment comes when we realize there can be no return, our exile continues to feel like a choice. The country where we were born was not our choice; we could have been born somewhere else. The process of growing up culminates with the realization that we are responsible for the choices we make.

At one moment we realize that our position is not unique, as we'd first thought. We are an individual functioning within a vast cultural text, which begins (depending, of course, on what you treat as the beginning) with the banishing of Adam and Eve from paradise. All that follows depends on interpretation. Was this paradise truly a paradise? Are Adam and Eve asylum seekers or exiles? Is there any difference? If they are banished from paradise because of the apple from the tree of wisdom does this mean that the place they found themselves in afterward is hell? Or vice versa? In the cultural text of exile we gradually discover the way complicated schemes work.

Contemporary feminists and literary theorists have taken on the theme of women and exile. The first who inspired me in terms of theory was Azade Seyhand with her book *Writing out of Nation*—her work on defining transnational literature. Other books came along later, which deepened the theme and expanded the reach of the research. The theme distanced itself from the perspective of the national literatures, except in cases of the generations of returnees—those who left Croatia after the Second World War, spent a lifetime in South America, and returned to relish the warmth of the homeland embrace.

I tripped over your sentence: "the thought consoles you that you can always buy a ticket and return *home*." Can you really return home?

It turns out that you cannot. And besides, the statistics confirm that true returns are rare. In *The Ministry of Pain* there is a little anthology of references to Croatian and Serbian nineteenth and twentieth century literature, mainly works that fictionalize the impossibility, the unsuccessful attempts and the tragedies of returning to what we think of as home. These books include Krleža's novel *Povratak Filipa Latinovicza* [*The Return of Filip Latinovicz*] and Miloš Crnjanski's *Roman o Londonu* [*A Novel of London*]. They also include the Yugoslav guest-worker novel *Kad su cvetale tikve* [*When the Pumpkins Blossomed*] by Dragoslav Mihailović, as well as Milovan Danojlić's *Dragi moj Petroviću*

[My Dear Petrović]—a novel about a returnee. That the "return to Eden" is not a theme that holds water is proved by the current realities of life, the life stories of those living scattered all over the world who rushed to Croatia at the outbreak of the war, guided by an array of motives. I don't know how all those stories ended, but I fear that their return to exile was more common than their permanent return to Croatia. A friend from Sarajevo recently sent me "Dođe naš ratnik iz rata u Grčkoj" ["Our Fighter Returned from War in Greece"], a poem by Ćamil Sijarić, which hit me like a blow to the solar plexus.

> *Our fighter returned from war in Greece*
>
> *And brought with him a Greek baking pan and, on his body,*
>
> *Wounds.*
>
> *Women told him the baking pan*
>
> *From Greece was no good, too shallow.*
>
> *We told him his wounds*
>
> *From Greece were also no good, too shallow.*
>
> *We told him:*
>
> *At home we would have inflicted deeper*
>
> *Wounds.*

Which works better for a writer (male or female)—exile or the cozy nest of a national literature? I see these as two diametrically opposed, but equally relevant, perspectives, two literary practices, two literary positions, two distinct artistic approaches, two different experiences, two different literary biographies, and, ultimately, two different truths.

How well can readers, critics, and defenders of the concept of national literature grasp the notion of transnational or postnational literature? Literature is definitely the most rigid of the artistic fields, it clings blindly to the national language and ethnicity as the sole valid proof that a literary work is Croatian, rather than Serbian or Bosnian. Languages change, disappear, reappear, and live on thanks to the principle of inclusivity, and die thanks to the principle of exclusivity. The language of literature tomorrow may be general and visual, new hieroglyphs, a more sophisticated or even simpler language of emoticons, a surprising combination of images and text. I continue to write in Croatian, not because I feel that my native language is the only valid language for literature. I found myself living abroad at an age when my cohort was making plans for retirement, and it was too late for me to start writing in another language.

In short, I feel not "lost" but "liberated" in translation. The new translation of *Štefica Cvek* into Bulgarian sounds absolutely *mine* and even better than the original *Štefica Cvek* does today in the new, changing Croatian linguistic, literary, and cultural climate. I experience the English versions of my essays as the most *mine*. What sent a colleague of mine back to the homeland was the moment when he realized he was relying on the English translation of his text more than on the text as he had written it in his native language. And this is the same thing that keeps me in exile and doesn't allow me to return to my so-called homeland. Exile has meanwhile become my domicile. My language and I—we haven't changed. And it's not that I fled into exile but that my former cultural community returned from its "coerced" political exile, from the "dungeon of peoples," from the "language dungeon," to its "primordial" homeland of Croatia. My former cultural community and I became irreversibly incompatible at many levels. All my nostalgia is gone, all my feeling for it is gone, there is barely anything left. Memory has been reduced to phantom pain, to wounds that are deeper *at home*. The inner pressure to remain on one's home turf, as well as the very idea of Croatian patriotism, are definitely, for me, socially pathological phenomena. Many will say I am criminalizing the idea of patriotism. Patriotism is, in practice, most often a criminal enterprise. Anyone who can convince me otherwise is welcome to try.

Yusef Komunyakaa claims that racism is a form of mental illness. Nationalism, too, is a form of mental illness. The ugliest of all "illnesses" is misogyny, though to treat misogyny as an illness is letting the misogynist off the hook. Why off the hook? Because a someone who is ill cannot be held responsible for their disease.

What tricks and strategies allow the *fox to survive?*

The fox as literary figure, symbol, and metaphor is packed with a wealth of meanings. The fox is the metaphoric guide for my novel of the same name, and I am author, huntress, and prey, all in one. I owe my choice of the metaphoric fox to "A Story about How Stories Come to Be Written" by Boris Pilnyak.

This story is the heart of the novel and the fox, its network of capillaries.

The fox is part of our general cultural heritage, she is a very old literary companion. In Western European literature the fox comes to us from folklore and Aesop's fables. The fox is the protagonist of the first European medieval novels (such as *Le Roman de Renard*). Slavic folk, oral, and literary forms favor the female gender for the fox. The farther we travel eastward, the richer and more complex becomes the character of the fox. She is a seductive woman, a sort of semi-deity. Her patron is Inari, the fertility goddess, and the fox is Inari's divine mail carrier, her courier. In Japan the fox is still a popular mythological figure and cultural archetype today. She has an ambivalent character, she can be evil, but she can also be good. First and foremost, she has superior intelligence. In some popular legends the fox lives a double life: by day she is a fox, by night, a woman. The fox is an outcast, a loner, hunted and hunter forever on the run. Her only trophy is a "rattle made of chicken bones."

In Chinese, Japanese, Korean lore, a fox requires a thousand years to become a serious deity and earn the greatest honor—nine tails! The tragic side of her character lies in loneliness, rejection, and a comprised biography (chicken thief!). The fox spends her time licking her wounds and worrying about the future of her offspring. The final chapter of my novel begins with a quote, a Bulgarian folk song about a widowed fox who bewails the fate of her kits. One of her young consoles her, singing: "Oh Mother dear, now don't you cry, you'll feed us easily by and by. Into the hunter's pouch we'll go, gracing the throats of the richest folk in the Sultan's white city of Istanbul." The art of survival (the trickster, the entertainer) implies a gruesome end. Foxes often do end up in the hunter's pouch, gracing the throats of the richest folk.

Why is the fox, so famed for her cunning and slyness, not better at improving her position and status? Because—and here we return to the metaphoric union of writer and fox—authentic writers are incapable of this and consequently they take upon themselves the risk of fall, defeat, and expulsion. There is a legend about a poor fellow who catches a fox. The fox turns into a woman overnight and turns back into a fox by day. The poor fellow knows that if he manages to steal her fur, the woman will permanently lose her chance of turning back into a fox. The woman, however, is happier returning to her wild, animal nature than she is to remain in conventional human form. The fox is like an alternate Eve who flees Eden, leaving Adam behind.

All in all, there are a number of answers to your questions and a number of interpretative options. Most readers will choose the perspective of the cultural cliché: the fox-woman writer is a liar, a shyster, a crook, a chicken thief. A minority will understand the dark, loser, fox/writer side. The fox knows that the only joy she can draw from her compromised life is ironic, hence the chicken-bone rattle. The real fox will prefer the fox's dream. For after a thousand years, the aurora borealis will glow on the divine horizon, the seductive Fata Morgana, those nine fox tails.

Can you map out women authors from these parts and/or from the world at large—their work, protagonists, perhaps their biographies—who had an impact on your writing?

I can, but as I contemplate doing so I wonder whether this isn't the work of literary critics, theorists, and historians. Somehow it seems as if most of those employed today in the literary realm are known for a lack of professional enthusiasm. Literature teachers in secondary schools and professors of literature at universities are growing lazy, as are students of literature. Editors are also growing lazy in publishing houses. And the writers themselves have grown lazy, having finally realized that lazy books sell far better than the nose-to-the-grindstone variety. True, one cannot call the fine literary critics, literary theorists, publishers, authors, agents, editors—the real enthusiasts—lazy. They are better said to have withdrawn, stepped back, gone underground. In their stead new, competent, market-oriented, multitasking enthusiasts are on the rise.

Who are these multitasking enthusiasts?

Multitasking enthusiasts with high-flung literary ambitions are the sleek, new market category in literary typology. With enthusiasm they rely on internet technology, social media, Facebook, Twitter, videos on YouTube, Instagram, and all the other accessible versions of "consumer" literature, from Kindle-only titles to audio books. Writers like these do not shrink from derivatives, if applicable, such as video games, comics, graphic novels, and so forth.

On the larger markets, the multitasking writer has a different impact than on the smaller, national markets. J. K. Rowling is a multitasking writer in that she has built a powerful industry based on her protagonist, Harry Potter. To be *marketable* is a relatively new category for valuing literature. These highly marketable authors are, as a rule, seldom seen in person. The publicity work and management of their careers is handled by paid professionals.

On the smaller markets, however, somewhat different forms of authorial positioning have evolved. Aside from activities related to modern technology (Facebook, Twitter, YouTube, Instagram, and so forth), multitasking writers employ strategies for all sorts of networking. By so doing they expand their fan base and increase the capital of their "intellectual" power. If someone stomps on their blisters, they resort to mobbing, just like teenagers in popular teen television series, or like local politicians. The multitasking writer reinforces their position in many ways and will never cut the branch on which they sit. They are sitting, after all, on many branches. The multitasking writer will not refuse television and televised public appearances, nor will they refuse participation in conversations about the most varied topics from ecology to the political situation in Belarus. Feminist orientated "regional" women readers will notice a remarkable brand-new phenomenon in the domestic literary constellation. Established writers, middle-aged or elderly, have become, ha, just a little edgy, like those high-ranking police officers who expect that any day now they will be caught red-handed in a lie or theft. Though the police officers, the guardians of law and order, are the least suspicious, everyone's turn comes up, we all steal and lie. Our literary police officer sees in contemporary female authors a quiet threat, for women are becoming increasingly visible and well read, and only they can threaten the police officer's high rank in the literary hierarchy. But if that literary hierarchy were to come tumbling down, and especially if women were to send it tumbling down, his life will lose its meaning.

There is a true story about a Serbian perfumer. In the early 1990s he began promoting a new perfume, bottled in a vial shaped like a hand grenade. The perfumer used the slogan: "Our bomb is a bomb of peace!" This was during the recent war. Why bring up this detail? Because this is the strategy embraced by the male literary arbiters as well. They began to do so aggressively, and, what do you know, began positively reviewing the books of contemporary women writers. In this way they hide their own incurable misogyny, precisely the way notorious drunks hide their alcoholism and the way the Serbian perfumer, mid-war, marketed his "bombs of peace."

And the strategy of our arbiters was transparent in matters of good and evil. When foreign women writers are in question, our arbiter hastens to provide a positive review of the books by these female authors who are already being glowingly reviewed the world over. Our arbiter assumes that domestic readers don't read foreign newspapers, and chances are he is right. When the arbiter is dealing with books by local women writers, however, he plays a more nuanced game and praises the books of those female authors who he believes to be at a far lower literary level than his. In other words, he'll praise those who, in his opinion, are not likely to jeopardize his position in the domestic literary hierarchy. Hence he, the arbiter, will cast his fishing line barbed with the hook known as women's rivalry, certain that he will snag readers, especially female readers, with his reviews. He will bestow on some authors a literary pedestal (though one that is a step lower than his own), while he'll declare all others—who are, thank goodness, still invisible—to be scribblers, churning out trivial, sentimental drivel, writing like a woman, these being a few of the condescending words and phrases used in English to disparage female authors. The Slavic languages, on the other hand, have a special arsenal of offensive language for female authors coined by punning on the words *pisati* (to write) and *pišati* (to piss). Insults particularly targeting women are *pisačica* (a cute wannabe female author) or *pišulja* (a female author whose writing is like piss). These words are used by the select few authors who have such a stranglehold on the media within the nationally structured literatures that nobody dares call them out for their discriminatory verbiage. And besides, since these words refer to women, to women writers, to scribblers, to pissy prose, nobody even notices the phrases or hears them as discriminatory. I have never read, or heard, of anyone referring to a male writer as someone whose writing was—piss.

And will the female colleague who is so honored renounce the pedestal bestowed upon her and opt instead for solidarity with the "pissy writers," or will she succumb to the seductive charms of the literary pedestal and her perch within the male literary hierarchy? Or not? Now there's a dramatic question for 100 euros.

I find myself recalling an episode from long ago. A female colleague and I were about to cross the street. We had the green light. A driver who was paying no attention to the traffic lights suddenly slammed on his brakes, nearly colliding with my colleague. He thrust his head out the window and blasted us with a salvo of curses. "I don't get why he is so angry," she said. "He didn't even run me over!"

The industry that produces millions of books will, ultimately, produce each year a dozen *relevant* titles. These dozen titles will be works of literature with high literary-aesthetic aspirations. Editors, translators, librarians, critics all take part in the global market homogenization, in assessing literary value. The venerable arbiters of good taste, critics like George Steiner, have all died. Their place has been taken instead, no holds barred, by writers themselves, hence it's the content providers who have taken control of the monopoly of judging the work of their peers, the other content providers. The term "content provider" is, in fact, the descriptor used in job searches for writers' positions in the creative industry.

A multitasking writer spends most of their time building their personal literary profile. The author's personal profile must be *marketable* for it to be the work of an author. If a writer like this claims in an interview that their literary mentor was Vladimir Nabokov, others step in and take over the mapping. They might also mention an intimate detail, such as a hobby (birdwatching, gardening, playing an instrument); taste in food (such as vegetarianism); a biographical detail (playing the drums in a rock band, for instance); their passion for sports (running a marathon); their religious, sexual, or political orientation. Marxism, for instance, is currently in. There, just the thing for our regional intellectuals, including writers, to resuscitate their Marxism in time and realign themselves. These fashions pass quickly. Most readers remember the authors, not their books (*Like you mean the guy who was running a marathon every day? Yes, that's the one, the writer from Japan . . .).*

And your own personal mapping?

I feel compelled in my books to remind readers of authors who have been, in my opinion, forgotten or left behind, as well as literary values that challenge the readers' horizon of expectations. An example of this sort of sabotage are the quotes I provide that refer to Eeyore, the plush donkey (from two novels, *Winnie-the-Pooh* and *The House at Pooh Corner,* by literary genius, A. A. Milne). Eeyore is the woebegone, endearing spirit behind *Thank You for Not Reading.* I'm delighted when readers (mainly the ones from non-Slavic countries) tell me how grateful they are for the books they have discovered thanks to my books. In *Europe in Sepia,* the quotes from Yuri Olesha's *Envy* give the collection its structure. I used the same strategy in *Nobody's Home.* There I use only quotes from *The Golden Calf* by Ilf and Petrov, while in *The Age of Skin,* I use quotes from Roma fairy tales and Croatian elementary school primers from the 1960s. In this I see my secret mission, in the subtle promotion of a perestroika of literary values. My strategy is hardly marketable, indeed, if anything, it is the opposite. One of my key criteria for choosing literary references is satisfaction with the text. As we know, however, readers find their own satisfaction. For most of today's readers, literature is merely a form of socializing—something like Facebook. The literary text is an opportunity for getting together, and anything can serve as an opportunity for socializing. Such readers read what others read. So this and this alone is why most of today's writers use Facebook. Facebook writers and a Facebook readership.

There is a legend about Stalin, who did not execute the Russian intelligentsia out of ignorance and caprice, but always first sought the advice of those who were better informed than he was. He summoned Pasternak and politely asked for Pasternak's opinion of Mandelstam. Pasternak answered obliquely that he and Mandelstam belonged to different poetic schools. And, oops, the next day Mandelstam was arrested and taken to a camp. I can only imagine how much simpler Stalin's job would have been had he had Facebook.

As far as the feminist side of mapping is concerned, my mother was responsible for my first feminist influences. She was a passionate reader who adored and collected books with women's names in the title: *Madame Bovary*, *Anna Karenina*, *Tess of the d'Ubervilles*, *Armance*, *Rebecca*, *Lucy Crown*, *Emma*, and many others. I did what I could to please my mother with *Štefica Cvek in the Jaws of Life* but did not succeed. Who knows, perhaps it is precisely because of my mother's criteria that the movie *Ninochka* is at the top of my list of favorite films.

There are three fragments in English on my website. One anticipates the possible disappearance of literature, literature as we have known it and know it still . . .

> Who knows, maybe one day there will no longer be
> Literature. Instead there will be literary websites. Like
> those stars, still shining but long dead, the websites

will testify to the existence of past writers. There will be quotes, fragments of texts, which prove that there used to be complete texts once. Instead of readers there will be cyber space travelers who will stumble upon the websites by chance and stop for a moment to gaze at them. How will they read them? Like hieroglyphs? As we read the instructions for a dishwasher today? Or like remnants of a strange communication that meant something in the past, and was called Literature?

How do you determine your model for writing?

I have said too much already. By speaking of self-determination I am underestimating my reader. Self-determination infantilizes the potential reader in a way and forces the author to use a patronizing tone. Sometimes I receive letters from readers asking me to answer similar questions. I am always touched by these requests but refrain from responding because they remind me of the phenomenon of "kiss feeding." Many animals (apes, wolves), mammals by and large, feed their young with food they have pre-chewed. Indeed, the traditional authoritarian education system relies on the principle of "chewing" (to chew on a subject!). This is how the future obedient "consumer" is trained to swallow what the authorities have pre-chewed for them.

I address a competent reader, a reader who would be more likely to have something to teach me than me to teach them. The key idea which continually inspires me is contained in a brief fragment of

Italo Calvino's "Whom Do We Write For? or The Hypothetical Bookshelf":

> [. . .] Literature is not school. Literature must presuppose a public that is more cultured, and *more cultured than the writer himself.* Whether or not such a public exists is of no consequence. The writer addresses a reader who knows more about it than he does; he invents a "himself" who knows more than he actually does, to that he can speak with someone who knows more still. Literature has no choice but to raise the stakes and keep the betting going, following the logic of a situation that can only get worse.

Self-determination is nothing new in literature, but market-oriented literature has turned this random sort of thing (depending on how individual authors relate to it) into a media spectacle. This spectacle is presented as a benevolent educational activity, although its function is purely market-driven. I am pleased when the way literature is determined comes from the literary underground. These are the blogs, podcasts, online magazines, where literary critics do not insist on seeing themselves as authors, where they write about literature as volunteers, out of appreciation, and least of all to promote their own plaudits as critics.

The melancholy of vanishing

How does this fit in with the idea that literature may, one day, cease to exist?

A new, modern breed has appeared of male and female authors who speak of themselves and their books with a mind-boggling self-confidence. There are more and more compatible, highly articulate "TED talkers" who can handle literary premastication with skill and seductive rhetoric. This combination of eloquence, intelligence, and breadth confuses me. I'd be prepared to sign off on everything this literary breed says without hesitation, but I am held back by a wariness I cannot explain.

I recently watched a video presentation by a well-known female author whose books have been translated into many languages, and whose sales are mind-boggling. She speaks English perfectly, looks terrific, is admirably eloquent, unerring in her communication with her audience. She is fluent in several languages, has degrees from two universities, lectures to students at prestigious schools, does not turn down functions at international literary organizations or juries for important literary prizes, or frequent appearances in political, cultural, literary, and other discussions.

She is an intellectual paragon. And on top of everything else she publishes at least one novel per year. She has everything in her rich thematic and ideological package: East and West (North and South); traditionalism and modernity; respect for several cultures; religions, gender, LGBT tolerance; respect for human rights; respect for (moderate) leftwing political options and a reticent empathy for the right; a world without violence; a robust ecological awareness; tolerance, tolerance, tolerance. The author, who also enjoys a successful private life (a mother, a happily married woman) recently announced that she is bisexual and with this intimate personal gesture, which goes beyond mere rhetoric, she proves her respect for various sexual orientations and earns a new readership. In the rich vocabulary of this successful writer the key word is empathy. Was it perhaps the word "empathy" that raised my hackles? Ever since we invented him, God has been promising us empathy as a matter of principle. Nobody, however, has found out from God how he translates this word into his language. Is it perhaps translated in the divine narrative as "pragmatic indifference"?

The woman writer with this strikingly attractive profile is not the only one such figure on the current literary landscape. She is a specimen of women's liberated self-confidence, a specimen of splendid self-management, successful self-implementation of the *know-how*, *know-what*, *know-who*, and *know-why* disciplines. Many savvy young women today are speedily mastering the intellectual and literary market. Hard-won female self-confidence has finally become sexy. Isn't that what we have always wanted? This fact ought to stir my celebratory enthusiasm, but, sadly, it does not. Perhaps I'm simply envious of my splendid female colleagues because I haven't managed to attain such a high level? Perhaps I'm upset by the realization that I have remained trapped in a time warp and am stubbornly waging a battle that has already been won? Perhaps multitasking writers are producing a new multitasking literature and new literary culture in which I probably will not take part. Just as I am unable to watch 3-D movies. They are too loud, visually aggressive, they insult me at the sensory level . . .

Can you clarify?

Please note that I didn't say literature will cease to exist, but that it *might* cease to exist, certainly as we know it now. If we are giving serious thought to the consequences of our relationship to nature, if we are thinking about global pollution, about technology, about the pending robotization, for instance, which will be taking jobs from millions of people, about the new forms of slave-holding, about pandemics, the era of post-truth, a new *transhuman* person, I don't see why we should stop short of examining one of the most venerable of human activities—literature. Perhaps literature will become transhuman! If it does, will I be ready as a reader, if not a writer, for this new literature? How will I react to the transplanting of the literary reception chip, for instance? Will my brain reject it? Might the future literary zone be off limits to me because of my lack of adaptability? Will I be technologically illiterate? Will I fail to get the password, or know where to find it?

And while we're on the subject of a possible future, there is a phenomenon known as "literary anticipation." In order to learn something about yourself you didn't know before, you need to start early with writing and write several books. As you age you begin to notice certain extra-literary elements, though literary anticipation is not something straightforward; it does not refer to something you invented, and then the something you invented actually happens a few years later. Here literature ceases to be literature and becomes the work of old-time fortune tellers. The work of old-time fortune tellers is, however, to tell stories, hence—literature. As the cook from the British television series *Downton Abbey* says: "Nothing in life is sure."

I should also say that authors do not become famous based on their anticipatory literary moments nor do these moments influence how their work is valued—what they have written is valued for other reasons. Anticipatory moments are usually valued in works of science fiction, utopia and dystopia, and in the genre of the speculative novel, as promoted by women such as Ursula K. Le Guin and Margaret Atwood, to name but two.

Yevgeny Zamyatin wrote the novel *We* in 1921. In it he describes a world that will only become real ten years hence under Stalinism. Zamyatin's novel inspired Aldous Huxley, the aforementioned Le Guin, Kurt Vonnegut, and especially George Orwell with his novel *1984*, which was published in 1949, almost thirty years later.

The anticipatory moment is not necessarily linked to the genre of the speculative novel; it is something that authors are usually not responsible for. The anticipatory moment is not a category for evaluating literature. This sort of thing is an instance of intuition or coincidence. Who can say which? Anticipatory fragments in someone's work—if they are recognized as such—are easily subject to appropriation by other authors (as in Zamyatin's case). Many people are fond of hunting stories (*I knew there would be war long before it began*—I heard many such comments from my former compatriots). *The Culture of Lies*, for instance, where I describe what was happening around me in the early 1990s, shows us today, thirty years later, that sadly very little has changed in the political and cultural landscape.

My first volume of stories, *Poza za prozu* [A Pose for Prose], particularly the novella "A Love Story," is a sort of fictionalized manifesto on gender relations in literature. "A Love Story" anticipates the theme of the gender aspect of literature that local female literary theorists have been working on. The collection was published in 1978 and today it has been completely forgotten. The same could be said for the novel *Štefica Cvek u raljama života* [*Štefica Cvek in the Jaws of Life*, included in the English volume, *Lend Me Your Character*]. Only the occasional belated translation into another language confirms the vitality of a literary text, as recently happened with its translation into the Bulgarian.

There is an eerie anticipatory moment in the book *Američki fikcionar* [*Have a Nice Day: From the Balkan War to the American Dream*, 1994; re-issued as *American Fictionary*, 2018] which came out in Croatian in 1993. There is a moment in the story "Shrink," where the narrator attends a therapy session and explains urgently to the American shrink that she is convinced that, having come to the United States from Yugoslavia, she has brought with her the virus of war, destruction, and chaos. Her greatest concern is for the Empire State Building. That was written in 1992. Then September 11th happened in 2001. A few months after the 9/11 tragedy, I shuddered when I thought back to that episode.

The anticipatory moment, I repeat, is not a category for valuing literature. It needn't manifest itself as a theme in the work, but may crop up in other elements, such as the structure, idea, or style. The anticipatory moment is a hidden, hard-to-explain node of energy. My books today are being read with a great deal of interest by young Spanish, US, Estonian, and other readers, many of whom have no idea that these books were written so long ago. These readers may not be numerous, but there are many more of them abroad than there are, for example, in Croatia. These time and place gaps are intriguing—the experience of seeing books travel over time and through different environments, as well as how the books are being read. The same can be seen with the revised second US edition of *American Fictionary*. The first edition had almost no critical reception, while the second edition has sparked far more interest. Perhaps the reality in the United States has caught up with my book. Or perhaps my book caught up with the reality in the US. Who knows.

Through many of your books runs the melancholy of vanishing. Is a happy literary outcome even possible?

I just read a report in the news about online auctions of the late Sylvia Plath's belongings. At one auction (*Your Own Sylvia*) a deck of tarot cards that Ted Hughes had given to Plath was sold for $200,000. The fifty-odd items sold at auction brought Plath's heir, Frieda Hughes, over $1,000,000. Among them was a particularly impressive rolling pin. Quite recently a Scottish miniskirt of Sylvia Plath's was sold at auction. The description of the skirt was much semantically richer than the reviews of the poet's poems had ever been: "The skirt represents Plath and her personality in every way—the conflict inside, her inner art monster, cloaked by the most precise, nearly persnickety, clothes. (. . .) Plath was miserable, but she created art, and the skirt is a representation of that struggle." I read these and other news items as if they are symbolic eulogies. Who actually died here? Literature died. At a moment when those who are nameless, the amateurs, the influencers, male and female, the politicians and porn stars, the writers and artists, the media gurus all become stars, when the genres of tell-all books, autobiography, and media-profiling have overshadowed the literary work, when *The Life and Work of X* is reduced to *The Life of X*, when what the author, male or female, wrote becomes irrelevant as long as their "product," their "work," refreshes the world and makes a difference, this is the moment when the death throes begin for the traditional concept of literature. If literature is to survive it must move into a zone of invisibility and go underground.

This moment seems the most narcissistic in the history of civilization. Today writers are writing their own hagiographies, or kickstarting their career by writing their own hagiography. In so doing they radically change the very essence of literature, even while being unaware of this, and mostly they are unaware. Consequently, they spur readers to write their own. And their readers have no need to tear their hair out over this—there are professional companies where nameless professionals are ready to tackle the job for them. Therefore, things are far deeper and more complex than they might seem at first glance. I won't be far off the mark, or so I hope, if I say that the key word in our contemporary vocabulary is—archive. More than a mere word, archive is diagnosis. Diagnosis is—to use an old term expunged from our current usage—weltschmertz, world pain, with unusual symptoms. We are all of us affected by a hysterical drive to leave traces of our personal existence on the planet Earth. This narcissistic hysteria is evaluated as a positive, as success, and, in the realm of literature, as artistic success. However, the Booker Prize has not appeased the anxiety of the successee, because in success the Booker has been far outstripped by the producer of little bottles filled with one's individual farts. Everyone has the right to leave their trace. Everyone is able to leave their trace. Traces draw attention to the fact that we exist, that we will not be erased. Therefore all evaluation is pointless, because the producer of fart jars and the author of a novel that has been awarded the Booker Prize end up equally forgotten. They will be pushed aside by a flood of new creative people, influencers, visual artists, writers, actresses selling candles perfumed with the scent of their own vaginas. They are all seeking, in a frenzy, the best possible way to leave a trace of their existence. Whence this fear of erasure, the possible disappearance of civilization? As far as literature is concerned, this fear has found its home in the genre that will be their salvation. Hagiography. Thanks to the indestructible wedding of democracy and digitalization, people can depart this world as saints. So it is that literature itself, in its mainstream, is being whittled down to a single genre, the hagiography (autobiography, autofiction), and so it is that the author, fraught by fear of disappearance, nullity, the loss of the importance of their work, the reduction of their efforts to laboring on an assembly line, step back from their text and become their own text. Their name matters more than the title of their work. Here I recall the statement of a serial killer who snorted in frustration: "Hey, how many times do I have to kill before I make it to the front page?!" Yet, who can guarantee that our lives are authentic? Who can guarantee that the saints really were saints? There is a weird company in Japan. Ingenious documentary-filmmaker Werner Herzog made the film *Family Romance* about it in 2019. The company provides an array of services. The client can hire people who will attend the funeral of a deceased who had no family. People can be hired to act as marital partners for those who need this kind of support (pornography, prostitution, sex are strict-ly prohibited). Werner Herzog zeroes in on the case of a little girl who has no father. Her mother contacts the *Family Romance* company. The owner spends time with the little girl, ultimately the girl opens up to him, begins to think of him as her real fa-ther. Her mother asks their rental dad to move in with them. The business owner refuses because this is not part of the deal. The end of the movie discloses a sad truth, the business owner is not part of the life of his own family. If his own family needs a father, they can only hire one.

Literature is not a toy in the hands of male or female writing egos. Literature must not (nor can it!) be placed under the control of national literatures, various ministries of culture, academies, pub-lishers and all those bureaucratic institutions that have latched onto literature with the excuse of giving it room to breathe, yet in fact seeing to its "esteemed" demise. Literature is communication between me and those of my readers who cannot be bought, no matter who and where they are. Recently a reader from somewhere in Chile messaged me to say he had COVID and was reading my novel, *Fox*. He is my authentic reader. How do I know? I simply do.

Literature is what happens between me and a reader I have never met somewhere in India who discovered something in my text that I wasn't myself aware of. Literature is what happens between me and a reader who showed up at a sparsely attended reading in Portland, bringing copies of all of my books that have appeared in English translations, and showed that he knew by heart the most minute details which I, myself, no longer remembered. We all of us depend on the "kindness of strangers" (*Whoever you are—I have always depended on the kindness of strangers*) like tragic Blanche from *A Streetcar Named Desire*. Literature is a non-utilitarian activity. But one *real* reader is enough to persuade me of the meaningfulness of my work. Mystical are the paths of literature.

And while we're on the subject of literary anticipation, Ray Bradbury's novel *Fahrenheit 451* and the unforgettable movie version, directed by François Truffaut, have been permanently etched in my memory. In the final scenes we discover the existence of a literary underground, hiding in a forest. Since possession of books is strictly banned in Bradbury's dystopian world, the book-people have chosen to live in a parallel world. This sort of scenography does not invoke vanishing but the inkling of a new life, of revolution. The book-people are members of an underground intellectual resistance movement, where each of them commits an entire book to memory. The book-people are living libraries. The only library that exists. Who knows, perhaps a reader will appear who will choose one of my books, thereby postponing my inevitable demise. Perhaps near the end of their life, this imagined woman-book or man-book will exhale my book into the mouth of someone else, and this person will, having lived their life, pass it on to yet another. Do I believe that in the very rhythm of inhaling and exhaling lies the meaning of literature? Is any other meaning necessary? Inhalation and exhalation—life itself. With the first breath it begins, with the last it ends.

(2021–2022)

Acknowledgements

My gratitude goes to Merima Omeragić without whom this book would never have happened. She provided the powerful impetus. And in the process, she shortened and simplified her questions so as to give me as much room as possible. She withheld her voice—as far as theoretical feminist literature is concerned. The editor and I gave up on categorizing this book in terms of genre—is this a conversation, an interview, or merely an unfettered monologue of mine? I fear it may be the third—but both of us know that Merima's voice as author, feminist and literary scholar has been unjustly sidelined. For the American edition I changed, redacted, and added, and for this I take sole responsibility.

For their helpful comments and support I wish to thank Ellen Elias-Bursać, Rada Iveković, Petar Milat, Zlatan Delić, Goca Smilevski, and Svetlana Slapšak, inexhaustible sources of female cultural optimism.

DUBRAVKA UGRESIC is the author of six works of fiction, including *The Museum of Unconditional Surrender*, and six essay collections, including the NBCC award finalist, *Karaoke Culture*. In 2016, she was awarded the Neustadt International Prize for Literature for her body of work. She went into exile from Croatia after being labeled a "witch" for her anti-nationalistic stance during the Yugoslav war. She lived in the Netherlands until her passing in March 2023.

ELLEN ELIAS-BURSAĆ has been translating novels and non-fiction by Bosnian, Croatian, and Serbian writers for thirty years, including writing by David Albahari, Neda Miranda Blazević Kreitzman, Ivana Bodrozic, Svetlana Broz, Slavenka Drakulic, Dasa Drndić, Kristian Novak, Djurdja Otrzan, Robert Perisic, Igor Stiks, Vedrana Rudan, Slobodan Selenić, Antun Soljan, Dubravka Ugresic, and Karim Zaimović.